Bringing Spanish to Life

C000246897

Bringing Spanish to Life provides an innovative and refreshing cross-curricular approach to teaching languages in primary schools, combining art, design and foreign languages with various aspects of the National Primary Curriculum such as literacy, numeracy and PE.

This unique practical resource comprises an engaging storyline about a day in the life of two Spanish children and gives an opportunity for learners to re-enact their day, using finger puppets, handmade crafts and exciting games to practise new language. Each of the fourteen sections begins with a short accessible dialogue in Spanish and is followed by suggestions for using the new vocabulary in pairs, small groups or as a whole class.

The main story is accompanied by fun craft activities linked to the story (one for each section, fourteen in total) for children to do in class using the templates and instructions provided. A wide range of further activities follows, consisting of lively games, songs and opportunities to communicate simple ideas. Language extensions are suggested, focussing on imaginative writing and reading ideas linked to the theme of each section.

Written to support the new foreign languages programme of study, the book includes:

- cross-curricular links to numerous subjects;
- classroom games and activities;
- photocopiable resources and templates for fun classroom activities and projects;
- language extension activities.

Bringing Spanish to Life can be read on three levels to suit a variety of classroom situations. First, the story can be told 'straight' with the whole class participating in the dialogues. Second, the story can be combined with the craft activities after each main section. Fourteen doing and making activities match the storyline and can provide a colourful, eye-catching display and learning focus in the classroom or for open days or assemblies. Teachers can use as many or as few as they wish. Finally, the language extension activities can be used alongside the craft activities as desired. The aim of these activities is to extend the target language in a relevant context through a variety of methods such as songs, playlets, simple communicative exchanges and games with numbers.

Catherine Watts is Principal Lecturer in the School of Humanities at the University of Brighton where she teaches German, English and Education. She co-authored with Hilary Phillips two *Living Languages* books published by Routledge in 2013 and two *Jumpstart!* foreign language books in 2014.

Hilary Phillips has been a class teacher in primary schools for over twenty years and was a Lead Teacher for Primary Languages in Brighton and Hove. She co-authored the *Living Languages* books, which describe innovative language learning projects in primary and secondary schools, and two *Jumpstart!* books containing over 400 engaging and exciting activities to teach languages in primary schools: *Jumpstart! French and German* and *Jumpstart! Spanish and Italian*.

Bringing Languages to Life

Bringing French to Life: Creative Activities for 5–11
Catherine Watts and Hilary Phillips

Bringing German to Life: Creative Activities for 5–11
Catherine Watts and Hilary Phillips

Bringing Spanish to Life: Creative Activities for 5–11
Catherine Watts and Hilary Phillips

Bringing Spanish to Life

Creative activities for 5–11

Catherine Watts
and Hilary Phillips

Routledge
Taylor & Francis Group

LONDON AND NEW YORK

First published 2015
by Routledge
2 Park Square, Milton Park, Abingdon, Oxon OX14 4RN

and by Routledge
711 Third Avenue, New York, NY 10017

Routledge is an imprint of the Taylor & Francis Group, an informa business

© 2015 Catherine Watts and Hilary Phillips

The right of Catherine Watts and Hilary Phillips to be identified as authors of this work has been asserted by them in accordance with sections 77 and 78 of the Copyright, Designs and Patents Act 1988.

All rights reserved. The purchase of this copyright material confers the right on the purchasing institution to photocopy pages which bear the photocopy icon and copyright line at the bottom of the page. No other parts of this book may be reprinted or reproduced or utilised in any form or by any electronic, mechanical, or other means, now known or hereafter invented, including photocopying and recording, or in any information storage or retrieval system, without permission in writing from the publishers.

Trademark notice: Product or corporate names may be trademarks or registered trademarks, and are used only for identification and explanation without intent to infringe.

British Library Cataloguing in Publication Data
A catalogue record for this book is available from the British Library

Library of Congress Cataloging-in-Publication Data
Watts, Catherine, author.
  Bringing Spanish to life: creative activities for 5–11/Catherine Watts and Hilary Phillips.
  p. cm
  Audience: Creative activities for 5–11.
  1. Spanish language – Textbooks for foreign speakers – English – Juvenile literature.
  2. Spanish language – Grammar – Juvenile literature. 3. Spanish language – Spoken Spanish – Juvenile literature. I. Phillips, Hilary, author. II. Title.
  PC4129.E5W45 2015
  372.656'1044 – dc23
  2014024428

ISBN: 978-1-138-79767-3 (hbk)
ISBN: 978-1-138-79768-0 (pbk)
ISBN: 978-1-315-75695-0 (ebk)

Typeset in Helvetica
by Florence Production Ltd, Stoodleigh, Devon, UK

MIX
Paper from
responsible sources
FSC® C013604

Printed and bound by CPI Group (UK) Ltd, Croydon, CR0 4YY

To all the children who have helped me craft these activities – thanks for all the fun!

CW

To Daryl, Kate and Gretel for all the fun we've had in primary languages

HP

Contents

Introduction: getting started

This book arose from all the fun we have had over many years making things with a wide assortment of primary-aged children to support our teaching. 'Why not combine these activities with foreign languages' we thought 'and have even more fun?' And so this book was conceived and we hope you enjoy using it as much as we have done writing it!

Who is this book for?

This book can be used by anyone interested in combining foreign languages with creative art projects that are fun to make and that practise foreign languages at the same time. Typical users of this book could be: primary-school teachers; parents/carers/grandparents looking for projects to do with their children over a holiday period; people running after-school clubs; home-school groups. The book is aimed primarily at young learners and is particularly relevant to the current primary-school curriculum where integrated learning leads the way and room has to be made for foreign languages in an already tightly packed timetable with effect from 2014. Whether you love making things, speaking and learning foreign languages or simply putting your heads together over something creative and motivating, this is the book for you!

About this book

We hope that this book will be a creative way to help children take up and use a new language. It tells a story written as a series of dialogues between two Spanish children, Daniela and Mateo López, about the events of a single day, going through everyday routines, shopping for a picnic in the park, etc. Children then make something connected with the story, which will help them to re-enact conversations of their own, starting with a finger puppet to represent one of the characters. A range of language-based activities follow that suggest ways to keep practising new vocabulary including role plays, songs and games.

A finger-puppet theatre is included at the end of Chapter 14, which the children can use with their finger puppets to act out the dialogues.

A dialogue form has been chosen so that it can easily be echoed, repeated and performed by groups or pairs of children in the classroom. It provides language in the first person (using the words *I* or *we*) so that children can simply lift the appropriate phrases from the text to express their own opinions. They are based around useful language that children can use when talking to other children through Spanish rather than their mother tongue in real-life situations. An English translation of each dialogue is provided at the back of the book. The story is flexible in form so you can dip in and out as it suits you, depending on how it fits in with other aspects of the curriculum.

First steps

First introduce the two main characters to the class (see *Introduction to children* on p. 3) and show children how to make their own finger puppet of one character using one of the templates provided. They will use these puppets to act out each dialogue and to be a prompt when they move round the room having conversations with other children. Using a puppet often helps children feel less self-conscious and more willing to speak through someone else's voice.

Next stage

The next stage is to read aloud each dialogue, adopting a different voice for each character (or asking a colleague to help) while children respond with an action with their puppet when their character speaks. Next time, children echo the words after you several times and then practise some of the phrases or exchanges with a partner. You can provide interest and variety by encouraging children to vary the loudness of their voices and their tone, for example making their voices sad, happy, afraid, excited, etc.

If you are working with beginners, listening, responding and speaking will be the key focus for your class throughout these dialogues. If your class is more experienced, you could introduce the written dialogues from the start as a reading exercise, but you still need to make sure that they have lots of practice linking the spoken and written word and many different opportunities to listen and repeat new vocabulary. The usual way to practise speaking is to encourage speaking in the safety and comfort of a whole class first of all, then to provide opportunities for partner or small group speaking and only then to ask or expect children to speak on their own.

Creative art

The first activity following the dialogue is always something for you and the children to make, such as a string of bunting, a dragonfly, a garden shed full of tools and so on. Detailed instructions are given first in English and then simplified into Spanish, allowing you to work at different levels and address the children in either language. More experienced learners might enjoy being language detectives, deciphering the Spanish sentences, collecting the verbs used and making up their own instructions for other events in the classroom. Full-scale, photocopiable resources make it easy to follow the creative art work, all of which are photographed for the colour-plate section of the book.

Using the language activities

There follows a bank of tried and tested language activities suggesting how you can introduce and practise new vocabulary. The first activities link existing knowledge to new vocabulary and suggest simple games often using picture flashcards. It cannot be stressed too much that children need to repeat and revise new words in a multitude of ways, so these games can be re-used at all stages of the book. The next set contains simple songs adapted to practise new phrases (no equipment needed except for your voices) and games where children can move or run around with a partner or group and have fun using the language in an active way. Finally there are role plays, surveys and more complex opportunities to explore new language.

Reading and writing in the language are the final stages in the process. Children could start by copying words or phrases to make labels and speech bubbles to attach to their models.

We have given opportunities in this book for further writing for more experienced learners, often scaffolded by the selection of phrases or sentences from the dialogues.

The fourteen chapters in this book can only provide a small number of activities. Many more can be found in *Jumpstart! Spanish and Italian* (Watts & Phillips, 2014) where you can find over 400 exciting ideas to introduce and develop language learning.

Curriculum links

At the end of the book we have provided some curriculum links that reinforce a cross-curricular approach to language learning and make it a more meaningful experience. Some links will be more appropriate to different year groups, and the life of the accompanying activities and materials may serve several year groups and provide an opportunity to revise essential vocabulary as children progress through the school.

Introduction to children: *¡Hola! ¡Hola!*

You are going to hear about two Spanish children Daniela and Mateo, their dog Luna and their family who live in Spain, and you will have a chance to act out what they say and do. First of all you're going to make a finger puppet of either Daniela or Mateo so that you and your friends can join in their conversations. In Spain children say *¡Hola!* to each other when they meet up instead of *Hello*. When you've made your puppet, have some fun and take it round the room and say *¡Hola!* to all the other puppets.

Note to the teacher/adult

There are two different templates for finger puppets that children could make to act out the dialogue. The first pair is more fiddly to make and would be more suitable for older children to colour in and use. Photographs of completed puppets are in the colour-plate section of this book as guidance.

Figure 0.1 Template 1: finger puppets (characters in the book)

Figure 0.2 Template 2: finger puppets (Luna the dog)

© 2015, *Bringing Spanish to Life*, Catherine Watts and Hilary Phillips, Routledge

Figure 0.3 Template 3: finger puppets (characters in the book)

Steps

1   Cut the finger-puppet templates out.
2   Add a face and colour the whole puppet in.
3   With Templates 1 and 2, glue tab A onto tab B making it tight enough to fit comfortably around your index finger. With Template 3, cut out the holes in the template and stick two middle fingers through to make a pair of legs.
4   Your puppets are now ready to use. *¡Pásalo bien! Have fun!*

© 2015, *Bringing Spanish to Life*, Catherine Watts and Hilary Phillips, Routledge

Acknowledgements

The authors and publishers would like to thank the following people for their help with both the text and the artwork in *Bringing Spanish to Life: Creative activities for 5–11*. Every effort has been made to contact copyright holders for their permission to reprint material in this book. The publishers would be grateful to hear from any copyright holder who is not here acknowledged and will undertake to rectify any errors or omissions in future editions of this book.

Grateful thanks are due to *Susana Prada-Garcia* (Lewes Old Grammar School) for helping us with the translations and final proofreading and *Daryl Bailey* (University of Brighton) for her timely advice and constructive criticism. We would also like to thank *Alex Chown* for all his practical help, suggestions and art work with the craft activities.

We are most grateful to *b small publishing ltd* for allowing us to design the artwork in Chapter 3 using their stencils (© b small publishing ltd.). The specific publication we have used is by *Clare Beaton* and entitled *Paper Dolls*. A range of delightful books and stencils, which are very reasonably priced, is available through www.bsmall.co.uk.

Our thanks are also due to *David Mostyn* (Oxford Designers & Illustrators) for illustrating each chapter so well.

Chapter 1 at a glance

Dialogue: this introduces the two main characters, Daniela and Mateo López, and their dog Luna, to you the readers. English translations of all the dialogues are included at the back of the book.

Language focus: simple greetings and responses

Creative art: make a paper bunting

Language activities

Activity one: practising questions and answers the fun way

Activity two: practising questions and answers with finger puppets

Activity three: greetings in a moving circle

Activity four: change your partner greetings

Activity five: sing a family name song

1 ¡Bienvenido a la familia López!

Welcome to the López family!

Daniela: ¡Hola! ¡Me llamo Daniela! ¿Cómo te llamas?

Mateo: ¡Hola! ¡Me llamo Mateo! ¿Cuántos años tienes? Tengo ocho años.

Daniela: Yo tengo nueve años. Vivo en España con mi madre, mi abuelo y mi hermano.

Mateo: ¡Tu hermano, soy yo! ¡Y mi hermana, eres tú, Daniela!

Daniela: ¡Sí, soy tu hermana! Y éste es el perro Luna.

Mateo: ¿Qué tal? Estoy muy bien. Estamos de vacaciones.

Daniela: Y yo, estoy muy bien. Me encantan las vacaciones. ¡Bienvenido a la familia López!

Creative art: make a paper bunting/*hacer las banderas*

A string of bunting is always fun to make and makes a fantastic decoration in your room. Use one letter on each flag and encourage each child to create at least one flag to help form a word or phrase in the dialogue (or indeed any other word), which they then contribute to the whole bunting. In a classroom, each table could make their own favourite new word to hang from the ceiling. Here are some examples from the first dialogue: *¡Hola!; ¡Bienvenido!; Me llamo . . .; la hermana . . .; las vacaciones.* A completed bunting is in the colour-plate section.

   Resources: coloured paper; scissors; glue; colouring pens/pencils; letter templates (optional as children can draw their own letters); bunting template; line of string; staples.

Figure 1.1 Letter template

© 2015, *Bringing Spanish to Life,* Catherine Watts and Hilary Phillips, Routledge

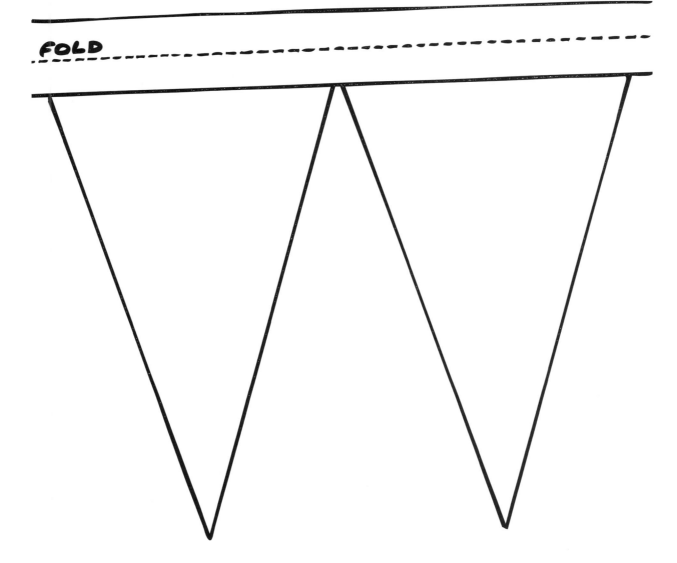

FOLD

Figure 1.2 Bunting template

© 2015, *Bringing Spanish to Life,* Catherine Watts and Hilary Phillips, Routledge

Steps

1 Photocopy the bunting template onto coloured paper and cut out the shape.
2 Do the same with the letters, making sure that each child has a selection to colour in and create a relevant word. Children can draw their own letters too instead of using the templates.
3 When the letters are decorated, glue one onto each flag until you have the complete word.
4 Glue (or tape) the flags together, keeping the top line as straight as possible.
5 Fold the top of the bunting over along the dotted line to make a cover for the string. Thread the line of string through the top of the bunting, secure with staples and display prominently! A photograph of a finished string of bunting is in the colour-plate section.

¿Cómo se hace?

Here are the instructions again, this time in simple Spanish. Use these if you are working with children in the target language.

1 *Cortad los triángulos.*
2 *Copiad las letras.*
3 *Coloread las letras.*
4 *Pegad las letras.*
5 *Pegad la cuerda.*

Language activities

Here are some key phrases based around the first dialogue that are used to greet other people and have a short conversation. They are very useful phrases and will help children get to know other children through Spanish.

Niño A (Child A)	Niño B (Child B)
¡Hola!	*¡Hola!*
¿Cómo te llamas?	*Me llamo . . .*
¿Cuántos años tienes?	*Tengo . . . años.*
¿Qué tal?	*Estoy muy bien, gracias.*

Activity one: practising questions and answers the fun way

Make an exciting start to your language learning. Use some of these techniques every time you introduce new phrases. Practise one set of greetings at a time, using the pattern of: you say, they repeat. Vary your voice each time, making it soft, loud, angry, questioning, gentle, shouting and so on, while the children echo your voice and tone. Clap out the rhythm of longer phrases, clicking your fingers or tapping your knees. Get the children up on their feet, waving their arms in the air as they chant or crouching down and gradually jumping up in the air as they finish the phrase. Make it fun to learn!

Activity two: practising questions and answers with finger puppets

Now the children use their finger puppets to ask each other the same questions and give each other an answer. Practise one set of greetings at a time.

Activity three: greetings in a moving circle

Children stand in two concentric circles making an outer circle and an inner circle. The inner circle turns around to face the outer circle and have an instant partner. They can now perform the following chant in unison facing their partner:

¡Hola!, ¡Hola!, ¿Cómo te llamas?

and the partner replies

Me llamo . . . ¿Y tú? (And you?)

After each exchange, the outer circle moves one step towards the next person on their left. If possible, shake hands with each partner or pretend to kiss him/her on each cheek. Try the same format with other questions.

Activity four: change your partner greetings

Children stand in a space with a partner or in a small group. Decide as a class which question and reply from the dialogue you will practise. In unison, each person shakes hands with one or more partners and asks the chosen question, replies in their turn and then everyone chants the numbers up to five together, turns to find another partner and repeats the same question. Make this speedy and lively.

Activity five: sing a family name song

Choose five children to hold up named picture cards of Daniela's family, for example, *la madre, el abuelo, la hermana, el hermano, el perro.* You can easily adapt the finger-puppet templates to make these characters. Everyone sings these names in display order to the tune of *London's Burning*.

La madre, la madre,

El abuelo, el abuelo,

La hermana, la hermana,

El hermano y el perro.

Each child holds their picture card up high when their card name is sung. Ask the children to change places at the end of the song to change the order for the next round. Finger puppets could be waved in the air too at the right time.

Chapter 2 at a glance

Dialogue: during the summer holidays Mateo wants to stay in bed, but Daniela has other ideas!

Language focus: telling the time and saying what you are doing

Creative art: make a paper plate clock

Language activities

Activity one: numbers 1–11 and *Bingo* game

Activity two: practising telling the time

Activity three: using their clocks to ask the time

Activity four: playing with numbers in a circle

Activity five: *What's the Time Mr Wolf?* game in Spanish

Activity six: linking times and actions

2 ¿Qué hora es?

What time is it?

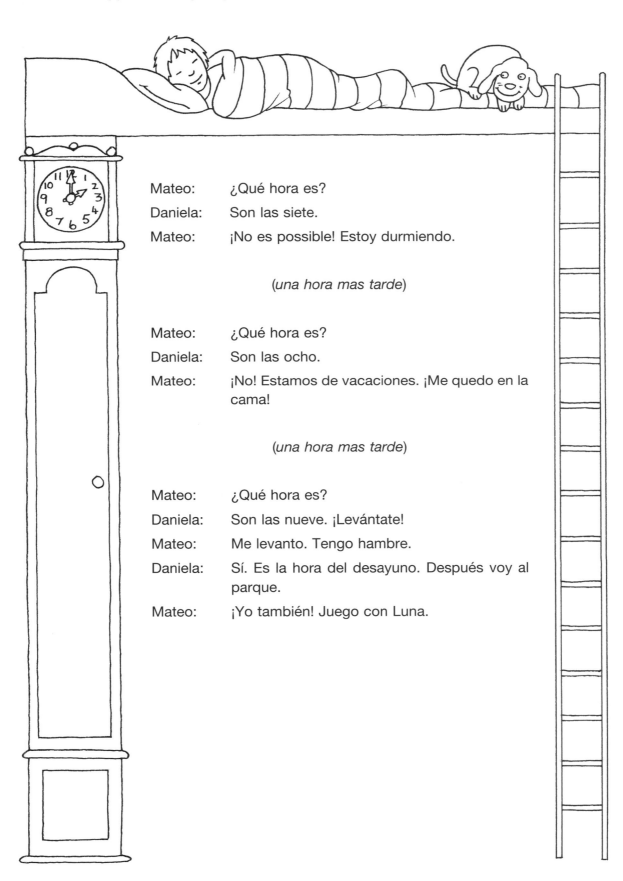

Mateo: ¿Qué hora es?

Daniela: Son las siete.

Mateo: ¡No es possible! Estoy durmiendo.

(una hora mas tarde)

Mateo: ¿Qué hora es?

Daniela: Son las ocho.

Mateo: ¡No! Estamos de vacaciones. ¡Me quedo en la cama!

(una hora mas tarde)

Mateo: ¿Qué hora es?

Daniela: Son las nueve. ¡Levántate!

Mateo: Me levanto. Tengo hambre.

Daniela: Sí. Es la hora del desayuno. Después voy al parque.

Mateo: ¡Yo también! Juego con Luna.

Creative art: make a paper plate clock/*hacer un reloj*

A clock face is simple to make and in this way the children can make up their own questions and answers using their own time displays. A completed clock is in the colour-plate section.

Resources per child: paper plate (any colour); butterfly pin (split pin); clock numbers (optional as children can draw their own) and hands (templates below).

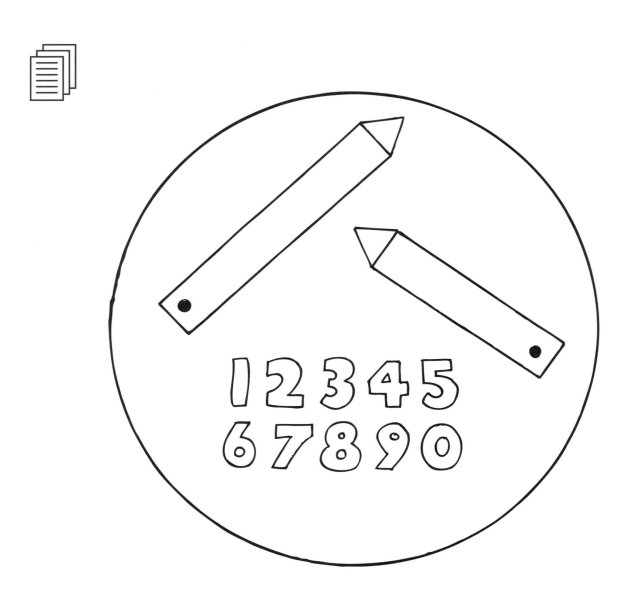

Figure 2.1 Templates: clock hands and numbers

© 2015, *Bringing Spanish to Life*, Catherine Watts and Hilary Phillips, Routledge

Steps

1 Photocopy the numbers, decorate them according to taste and place them around the edge of the paper plate to make the outer rim of the clock. Alternatively, the children can draw their own numbers directly onto the paper plate.
2 Give each child a pair of clock hands. Decorate these too.
3 Make a small pinhole in the centre of the plate and one on each of the clock hands indicated by the black dots.
4 Push a butterfly pin (split pin) through both clock hands and the centre of the clock. The long hand should lie below the short hand. A photograph of a completed clock is in the colour-plate section.

¿Cómo se hace?

1 *Copiad los números.*
2 *Decorad los números.*
3 *Haced lo mismo con las agujas del reloj.*
4 *Haced un pequeño agujero en el centro del plato.*
5 *Pegad las agujas.*

Language activities

Activity one: numbers 1–12 and *Bingo* game

Learn and practise numbers up to twelve: *uno*; *dos*; *tres*; *cuatro*; *cinco*; *seis*; *siete*; *ocho*; *nueve*; *diez*; *once*; *doce*. As before, practise numbers speaking loudly/softly alternately or making your voice happy/sad/low/high. Point from one side of the room to the other to count numbers and/or jump in the air every second number. Keep the activity fast and lively. Play *Bingo* with a selection of the numbers. Ask the winner to read back their numbers in Spanish.

Activity two: practising telling the time

Make a list of the hour times based on the examples in the dialogue such as: *son las siete*; *son las ocho*, etc. Move on to introduce other hour times. Watch out for *es la una* for one o'clock. Twelve o'clock is *son las doce* but you could distinguish between *es mediodía* (midday) and *es medianoche* (midnight). Use a clock face to show the time and ask the children to call out the Spanish phrase. Play this game in reverse: you call out the Spanish and they show the correct time on their individual clock faces.

Activity three: using their clocks to ask the time

Children take their clocks around the room and ask each other the time, giving answers in return based on the exchanges in the dialogue, for example:

Child A: *¿Qué hora es?*

Child B: *Son las nueve.*

Activity four: playing with numbers in a circle

Children stand in a circle. Give out lots of number cards up to twelve (or a higher number if appropriate) randomly around the circle. Count aloud in numerical order briskly. The children hold up their number when it is called. Now count in reverse order from the highest number downwards and the children again hold up their number when it is called. Count again around the circle but this time following the random order of the cards in the circle asking each child to hold up their card in turn. Do this lots of times with the children doing different actions on each rotation such as jumping in the air, crouching down, spinning around, all whispering and then shouting their own number, etc.

Activity five: *What's the Time Mr Wolf?* game in Spanish

Play a Spanish version of *What's the Time Mr Wolf?* One person (*Señor Lobo*) stands at the end of your room or hall and turns their back on the class. The children slowly and furtively creep up, asking in unison *¿Qué hora es, Señor Lobo?* S/he replies with an hour time until the stage when s/he calls out *¡Es medianoche!* and chases them away.

Activity six: linking times and actions

Make a list from Dialogue 2 of the children's activities and alongside them all the possible times, for example, *Estoy durmiendo; son las siete*. Invite the children to put together as many combinations as they can that seem sensible and then encourage them to create some silly sentences such as *Voy al parque, es medianoche*. The children could recite their favourite in pairs to the class or make up a collection for a display alongside their clock faces. More ambitious groups could add the half hour, for example, *son las dos y media, son las cuatro y media.*

Chapter 3 at a glance

Dialogue: Mateo and Daniela get washed and dressed

Language focus: talking about the clothes you are wearing, different colours and actions

Creative art: dress a puppet

Language activities

Activity one: talking about colours

Activity two: *Touch the Colour* game

Activity three: talking about colours with puppets

Activity four: *Traffic Lights* game

Activity five: holiday clothes suitcase

Activity six: *Get Ready* game

3 Me levanto

I get up

Daniela:	Me levanto y me lavo las orejas.
Mateo:	Y yo, me lavo los ojos y la nariz.
Daniela:	¡Y después lávate las manos!
Mateo:	Sí, me lavo las manos. ¡Y tú, lávate los pies!
Daniela:	Claro, me lavo los pies. ¡Cepíllate los dientes!
Mateo:	Sí, me cepillo los dientes. ¡Y tú, cepíllate el pelo!
Daniela:	Sí, me cepillo el pelo. Y ahora me visto. ¡Ponte tus pantalones cortos, Mateo!
Mateo:	Me pongo mis pantalones cortos azules y un jersey rojo.
Daniela:	Y yo, me pongo los pantalones cortos verdes y una camiseta amarilla. ¡Vámonos!

Creative art: dressing up/*vestirse*

Designing your own wardrobe and decorating the items to wear is always good fun. With these two models, children can create the clothes to wear – all in Spanish of course! A finished pair of dressed-up people are in the colour-plate section.

Resources: people cut-outs to dress; items of clothing to attach to the figures; pictures from magazines/the internet for the faces (optional); glitter, sequins, feathers, stickers, etc. with which to decorate the clothing; adhesive putty; colouring crayons and marker pens.

Useful vocabulary

clothes	*la ropa*	shirt	*la camisa*
trousers	*los pantalones*	shorts	*los pantalones cortos*
skirt	*la falda*	dress	*el vestido*
pullover	*el jersey*	t-shirt	*la camiseta*
coat	*el abrigo*	hat	*el sombrero*
scarf	*una bufanda*	boots	*las botas*
slippers	*las zapatillas*		

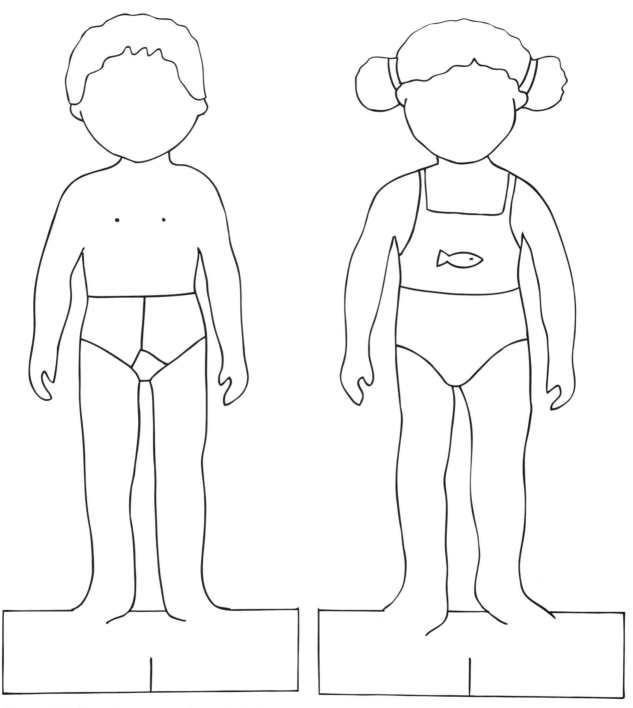

Figure 3.1 Templates: people and clothes

© 2015, *Bringing Spanish to Life*, Catherine Watts and Hilary Phillips, Routledge

Figure 3.2 Templates: people and clothes

© 2015, *Bringing Spanish to Life*, Catherine Watts and Hilary Phillips, Routledge

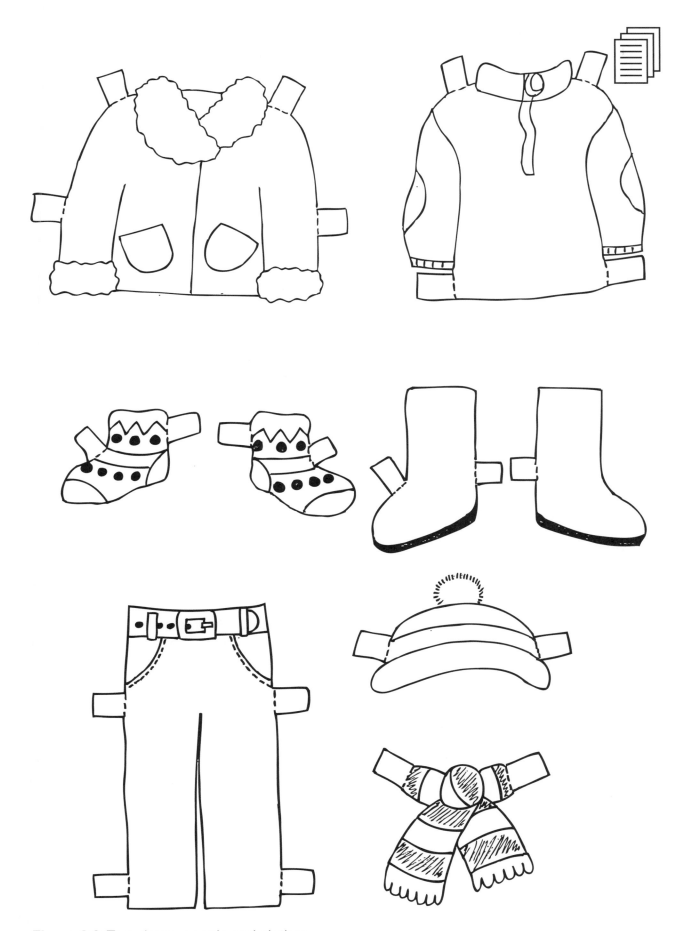

Figure 3.3 Templates: people and clothes

© 2015, *Bringing Spanish to Life*, Catherine Watts and Hilary Phillips, Routledge

Steps

1   Copy the models onto cardboard and cut out the shape around the solid line.
2   Children choose a figure to work with. Draw in their own faces or that of their partner, or use cut-out faces from magazines/the internet.
3   Select items of clothing they will use from a central table. They could ask for them in the target language, for example *una camisa por favor* using the vocabulary above.
4   Colour in and decorate the figures and clothes.
5   Cut the clothes out along the solid lines.
6   Fold back the tabs on the clothes along the dotted lines and use adhesive putty or a small dab of glue to secure the clothes onto the figures more firmly if necessary.
7   Stand the dressed figures up by folding back the dotted lines on the base. You could glue a drinking straw up one leg and up the back/neck of the figures on the reverse side to give the figures more stability.

¿Cómo se hace?

1   *Dibujad el cuerpo.*
2   *Dibujad la cara.*
3   *Escoged los vestidos.*
4   *Coloread el modelo.*
5   *Pegad los vestidos.*

Language activities

Activity one: talking about colours

Hold up cards of different colours and teach common colours, for example: *rojo* (red); *amarillo* (yellow); *azul* (blue); *verde* (green); *blanco* (white); *negro* (black); *naranja* (orange). Teach and practise the question: *¿De qué color es . . .?* (What colour is it?). Point to items in the room you are in and ask *¿De qué color es eso?* Children respond with *es azul, es verde,* etc. Invite a confident child to take your place and ask the question and then children do the same thing in pairs.

Activity two: *Touch the Colour* game

Put some colour cards around the room on the walls. Call out a colour name and children run to the correctly coloured card. Put up more than one card of each colour to prevent a crush!

Activity three: talking about colours with puppets

Children take their dressed puppet around the room and ask each other the question *¿De qué color es eso?* pointing to their model expecting an answer *es azul,* etc.

Activity four: *Traffic Lights* game

Play *Traffic Lights* using the basic colours of red/*rojo* (for 'stop'), green/*verde* (for 'go'), orange/*naranja* (for 'get ready'), yellow/*amarillo* (for 'accident' i.e. everyone lies on the floor). Start with the children standing in a space in a 'traffic line'. Call out a colour name and show the colour card to get everyone to move. Add some of your own colours for fun and make up a suitable action, for example, emergency vehicle racing.

Activity five: holiday clothes suitcase

Put up pictures of different clothes in different colours. Practise saying some basic clothes names, for example, *los pantalones cortos, una camiseta, un jersey, los pantalones*. Children draw a suitcase shape and draw inside five or six examples of clothes to take on their summer holiday, which they label in Spanish. They could add the colour name after the clothes name such as *un jersey rojo, una camiseta roja*.

Grammar note: colours are always placed after the noun in Spanish and if they end in *o* in the masculine singular, they should change to *a* if the noun is feminine, *as* for feminine plural and *os* for masculine plural as in *una camiseta blanca, unas camisetas blancas, un sombrero blanco, unos sombreros blancos*. Be careful too with colours that are originally the names of *things,* such as orange/*naranja* or pink/*rosa* as they only change in the plural. *Verde* changes only in the plural as well.

Activity six: *Get Ready* game

Collect from the dialogue some of the actions done in the morning by the children, for example: *me lavo las manos*; *me pongo los pantalones cortos*. Practise saying these phrases with suitable actions. Then play the *Get Ready* game. You all call out together *uno, dos, tres* and you alone call out one of the actions such as *me lavo las manos*. Children mime the action as they hear it. Try to foster suspense and encourage drama.

Chapter 4 at a glance

Dialogue: Mateo and Daniela talk about what they like to eat and drink

Language focus: likes and dislikes in the context of food

Creative art: make a fruity milkshake

Language activities

Activity one: using key phrases to express likes and dislikes

Activity two: saying what you like and dislike to eat for breakfast

Activity three: *Fruit Salad* game

Activity four: practising questions and answers around the room

Activity five: using connectives to link likes and dislikes

Activity six: song about food

4 El desayuno

Breakfast

Daniela: ¿Qué hora es?

Mateo: Son las nueve. Es la hora del desayuno. Tengo hambre.

Daniela: Y tengo sed. Bebo chocolate caliente y como pan tostado.

Mateo: No me gusta el chocolate caliente. Bebo leche. ¡Soy un monstruo de la leche!

Daniela: ¿Te gustan los cereales?

Mateo: Sí, me encantan los cereales. ¿Te gustan los churros?

Daniela: No, no me gustan churros. Prefiero los bocadillos.

Mateo: ¡Buen provecho!

Breakfast information: churros are long thin strips of doughnuts that people like to eat for breakfast and dip into a cup of hot chocolate.

Creative art: make a fruity milkshake/*hacer un batido de frutas*

Milkshakes are a tasty treat and the recipe below is straightforward and child-friendly. No cooking is involved and the healthy ingredients are easy to prepare. Before you start you need to collect up the following utensils: a chopping board; knives; an apron; spoons; a bowl; a liquidiser; drinking straws and glasses.

Steps

1   Prepare your food-preparation space with a suitable table covering.
2   Wash hands before starting.
3   Read and decipher the Spanish ingredients list together. Keep the English translation to one side until you have worked through the list.
4   Encourage the children to work as a language detective with the Spanish version of the recipe and instructions and use the English only as a fallback.

Make a milkshake   ## *Hacer un batido*

Strawberry milkshake

Ingredients

Half a litre of milk
Three very ripe pieces of fruit from
a choice of a banana, a peach or a
nectarine, six strawberries, a small mango

Un batido con fresas

Los ingredientes

Medio litro de leche
Seleccionad tres frutas maduras de
entre éstas: un plátano o un melocotón
o una nectarina, seis fresas o un mango
pequeño

Steps

1   Rinse the fruit and cut into chunks.
2   Put all the chunks into a liquidiser.
3   Add the milk and mix well.
4   Pour the mixture into a big glass.
5   Decorate with strawberries cut in half.
6   Sip with a straw!

¿Cómo se hace?

1   *Enjuagad y cortad la fruta.*
2   *Poned la fruta en una licuadora.*
3   *Añadid la leche y mezcladla.*
4   *Servid la mezcla en un vaso grande.*
5   *Decorad con fresas.*
6   *Bebed con una pajita.*

   ¡BUEN PROVECHO!

Language activities

Activity one: using key phrases to express likes and dislikes

Teach the very useful verb to express liking/disliking from Dialogue 4 *me gusta/me gustan* and ask children to look for its opposite *no me gusta/no me gustan*. Practise these verbs orally by repeating them over and over again in a little rhythmic chant for the class to join in, slapping their knees, moving their arms in the air, swaying from side to side, etc. These verbs will be some of the most useful vocabulary they will learn, so they need to master them. Mime a tennis game against the class by pretending to hit a ball in a dramatic way and calling *me gusta*. They return the mime in a similar way with *no me gusta.*

Activity two: saying what you like and dislike to eat for breakfast

Put up some pictures of breakfast foods and drinks mentioned in the text and make some combinations of likes/dislikes with these food items such as: *me gusta el chocolate caliente; no me gusta la leche*. As before, you call out the positive *me gusta . . .* and children reply with the negative *no me gusta . . .*

Grammar note: in Spanish remember that if you are saying you like or don't like something singular (for example milk, chocolate) you use *me gusta/no me gusta*. However if you say you like or don't like something which is plural (such as apples, bananas) then you use *me gustan/no me gustan*. Finally, notice the unusual order of words and keep the food/drink item at the end of the phrase.

Activity three: *Fruit Salad* game

Play a *fruit salad* game with four of the simplest food/drinks, for example, *la leche, el chocolate, el pan, los churros*. Children stand in a circle. Give each child in turn one of the food/drink names to remember and then call out one food item. All the children with that item run into the middle of the circle and change places with each other. To add extra fun, give them an incentive for good behaviour. Call out *el desayuno* and they all get up and change places. Use this sparingly and it works well as a reward.

Activity four: practising questions and answers around the room

Practise the question form *¿Te gusta . . .?/¿Te gustan . . .?* and make sure that everyone is confident about responding either *me gusta/me gustan* or *no me gusta/no me gustan*. Each person works out a very simple question such as *¿Te gusta el chocolate?* or *¿Te gustan los churros?* All the children get up and move around the class asking each other their questions and receiving a positive or negative reply, such as *sí me gusta el chocolate* or *no me gusta el chocolate* or *no me gustan los churros.*

Activity five: using connectives to link likes and dislikes

Look back at the positive ways to express likes, for example, *me gusta la leche* and then the negatives such as *no me gusta la leche*. Ask children to use the connective *pero* meaning *but* to join together something they like and something they dislike as in the following example: *me gusta la leche pero no me gusta el chocolate.* Children could then make a poster containing these sentences about breakfast foods with pictures that they could draw or cut from magazines.

Activity six: song about food

A little song is not hard to learn in a foreign language as long as the words are simple and the tune is familiar. Teach the song below one line at a time or divide the class into groups to sing one line each. Encourage the children to sing the song through twice to get a confident sound and then add some suitable actions.

To the tune of *Three Blind Mice*:

Me gusta la leche x 2 (both thumbs up)

No me gustan los churros x 2 (wag index fingers)

Me gusta el pan, me gusta el té x 2 (big smiles)

El desayuno x 2 (both thumbs up)

Chapter 5 at a glance

Dialogue: Mateo and Daniela prepare a picnic and buy some food items in the market

Language focus: talking about food

Creative art: make a picnic basket

Language activities

Activity one: practising numbers and food

Activity two: team game about food and prices

Activity three: food relay game

Activity four: shopping role play

Activity five: team game about healthy/unhealthy foods

Activity six: make a poster display

5 El picnic

The picnic

Abuelo:	Buenos días Mateo. ¿Qué tal? ¿Dónde vas?
Mateo:	Muy bien abuelito. Voy al parque con Daniela y Luna a hacer un picnic.
Abuelo:	Toma diez euros para comprar un picnic. Uno, dos, tres, cuatro, cinco, seis, siete, ocho, nueve y diez euros.
Mateo y Daniela:	Muchas gracias, abuelito. ¡Vámonos! ¡Hasta pronto!

(al mercado)

El tendero:	Buenos días, niños. ¿Qué queréis?
Daniela:	Buenos días, Señor. Quiero dos manzanas por favor.
El tendero:	¿Algo más?
Mateo:	Dos plátanos, por favor.
El tendero:	¿Algo más?
Daniela:	Dos tomates, por favor.
El tendero:	¿Algo más?
Mateo:	Dos pasteles de fresa y dos Coca Colas por favor.
Daniela:	¿Cuanto cuesta, por favor?
El tendero:	Cinco euros.
Daniela:	Aquí tiene. Gracias. ¡Adiós!

Creative art: make a picnic basket/*hacer una cesta de picnic*

A picnic basket makes a colourful display, especially if it is filled with picnic foods labelled in Spanish. A completed basket is in the colour-plate section.

Resources: two sheets of differently coloured, A4-size, thick paper or cardboard per child; scissors; pencils; ruler.

Steps

1   Cut eight strips for each child from the paper or card. Each strip should be 28 cm long by 1.5 cm wide. If you make four strips from one colour and four from the other, your basket ends up looking really smart!
2   Place four strips side by side on a flat surface. Weave in the remaining four.

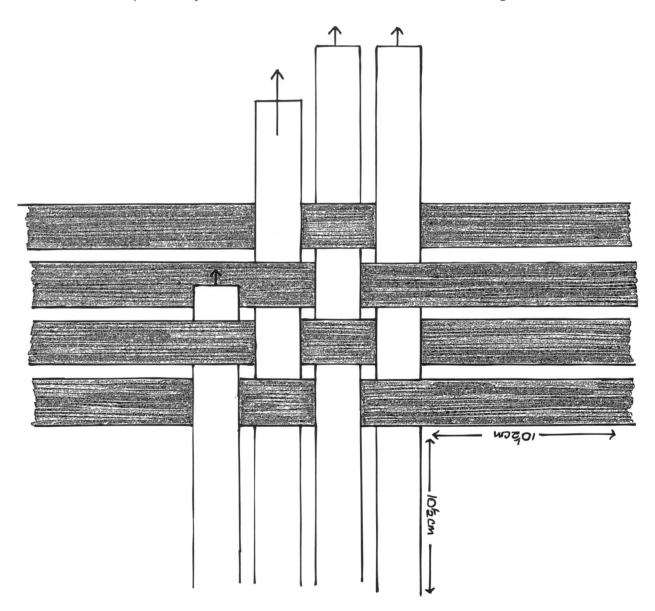

3   Fold up all the ends to make the side frames of the basket. Try to fold each strip straight up, i.e. at right-angles to the one below.

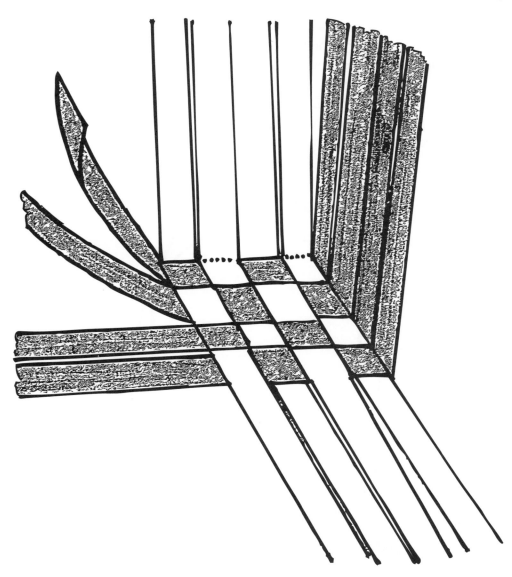

4   Now cut four more strips of coloured paper/card to the same dimensions as before, i.e. 28 cm long by 1.5 cm wide. Weave these in and out of the upright spokes. Start weaving each new strip at a different corner to give some stability to your basket. Note: you can hold the strips in place with a paper clip.

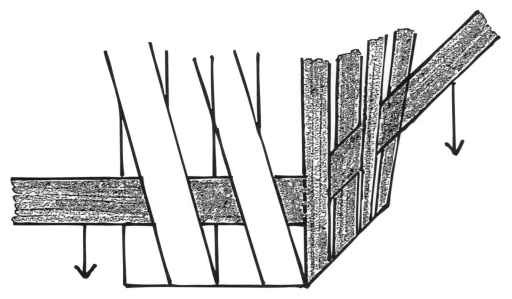

5   You can fold each strip into quarters to make the weaving easier as you place the strip over the uprights and lower it down. The higher up the basket you weave, the easier it gets!

6   When all four strips have been woven in, trim the ends and tape them to the inside of the paper basket.

7   Finally you need to add a handle. Cut another strip of coloured paper/card, this time 25 cm by 1.5 cm, and tape one end to the inside of the basket, roughly in the middle of the top row of weaving. Do the same on the other side.

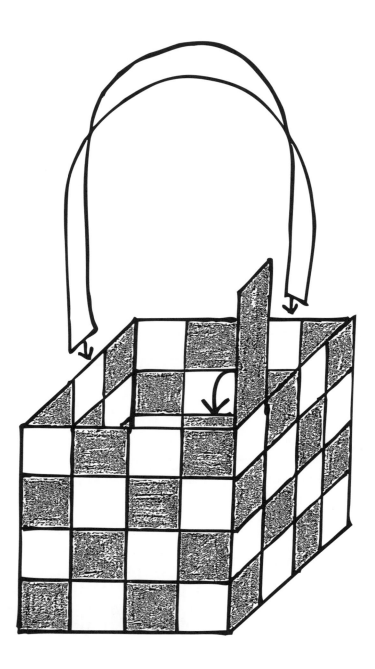

8   Now fill your picnic basket with some lovely things to eat and drink (either plastic food or else drawn by the children) and label each item in Spanish. Hang your baskets on a line across the room for everyone to see!

¿Cómo se hace?

1   *Cortad ocho pedazos de papel.*
2   *Trenzad los papeles.*
3   *Doblad los papeles.*
4   *Pegad los papeles en el interior de la cesta.*
5   *Colocad el asa en la cesta.*

Language activities

Activity one: practising numbers and food

Put up some pictures of food from the text, for example, apples, bananas and tomatoes, and practise their Spanish names. Then quickly flip through the pictures and ask children to call out the names as fast as they can. Attach a number to each picture and have children call out the whole phrase such as: *dos naranjas*; *cinco tomates*.

Activity two: team game about food and prices

Add a Post-it to the corner of each picture with a price on it in euros. Divide the class into two teams: one team has to call out the food name, for example, *dos tomates* and the other team has to call out the price. Swap over teams after a couple of turns. Then turn the cards over so that nothing is visible. Try again from memory! Ask the whole class to call out the question: *¿Cuánto cuesta?* (How much is it?) before the price is called.

Here's an example: *dos tomates. ¿Cuánto cuesta? Tres euros.*

Activity three: food relay game

Children sit in pairs down the centre of the room, legs stretched out to touch their partner's feet like a ladder. You may need to make two ladders to fit everyone in. Check that feet are on the floor safely, that no knees are poking up and that there is space to run between the pairs. Give each pair a price, for example, *dos euros* or a food such as *dos manzanas* and then call out each price or food at random. The called pair has to run up to the top of the ladder through the feet and back down the sides to their place as fast and safely as possible. Note: try to keep a tally of the prices/foods you have already called as it is easy to lose count.

Activity four: shopping role play

A shopping role play is a popular activity and very adaptable. Divide the children into two teams; one set of shopkeepers (*los tenderos*) and one set of shoppers (*los clientes*). If possible, children could draw pictures of their wares in their shop or use plastic food items but, if there is no time, imagination will be enough. The shoppers circulate and ask for different quantities of food and drink while the shopkeepers remain at their shop position and have to serve their customers, using the vocabulary from the dialogue as much as possible as a prompt.

Activity five: team game about healthy/unhealthy foods

Introduce the phrases *es bueno para la salud* – it's good for your health, and *es malo para la salud* – it's bad for your health. Practise these by chanting them with a regular rhythm and tapping hands together to remember the shape of the phrase. Divide the children into two groups and show pictures of some food already learned. One side has to name the food in Spanish and the other side calls out the relevant healthy/unhealthy phrase. Continue with a confident child coming to the front and acting as one of the two sides or playing the game in pairs or with all children moving around the room and asking each other to name a card and say if it is healthy or not.

Activity six: make a poster display

Design a poster together on a piece of A3 paper with pictures of food items on the left labelled in Spanish and prices with the healthy/unhealthy statement on the right.

Chapter 6 at a glance

Dialogue: Mateo and Daniela meet their cousin Diego on the way to the park. It is Diego's birthday today!

Language focus: talking about ages, months of the year and birthdays

Creative art: make a pop-up (birthday) card

Language activities

Activity one: *Happy Birthday to You* song

Activity two: months of the year

Activity three: *Birthday Runs* game

Activity four: talking about birthday dates

Activity five: make a balloon display

Activity six: class birthday chart

6 ¡Feliz cumpleaños!

Happy birthday!

Daniela:	El parque está cerca de aquí. ¡Mira, Mateo! Aquí está nuestro primo, Diego.
Diego:	¡Hola Daniela y Hola Mateo! ¿Qué tal?
Mateo:	Muy bien gracias. ¿Es tu cumpleaños hoy?
Diego:	Sí, es hoy, el tres de marzo.
Mateo:	¿Cuántos años tienes?
Diego:	Tengo diez años.
Mateo:	No tengo una tarjeta de cumpleaños para ti. Lo siento.
Daniela:	Pero tenemos un pastel de fresas con una vela.
Daniela y Mateo:	¡Feliz cumpleaños!
Luna:	¡Guau! ¡Guau!

Creative art: make a pop-up card/*hacer una tarjeta pop-up*

Everyone likes to receive a greetings card and it is both motivating and fun for children to be able to make them and send them in a foreign language! There are so many occasions when sending a card is appropriate, for example all the usual holidays, but don't forget about *World Hello Day* and the *European Day of Languages* as well as birthdays and other family days. Here is a simple pop-up strip card that does not require a template. A finished card is in the colour-plate section.

Resources: A4-sized white paper or thin cardboard; colouring pencils/felt pens; glue; scissors.

Steps

1   Take two pieces of A4-sized paper or thin white cardboard. Fold each piece in half and put one piece aside.
2   In the middle of the folded edge of one of the pieces of paper, mark two crosses one centimetre apart.
3   Starting at the dots, draw two parallel lines out towards the middle of the paper but only 2.5 centimetres long.
4   Cut along the lines starting from the folded edge.

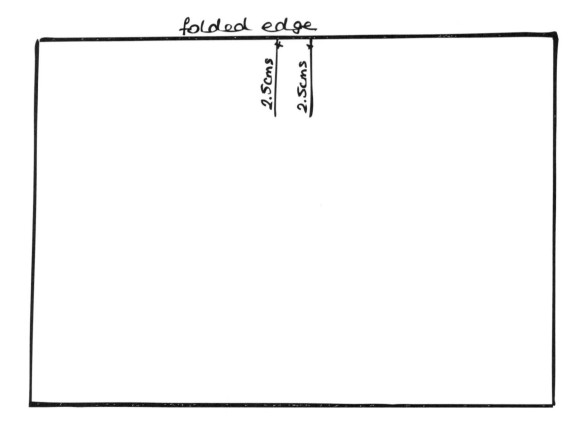

5   Fold the cut strip back and then fold it forwards again. Push the strip through to the other side of your card. Close the card and press firmly. Open it up again to see the little pop-up strip.

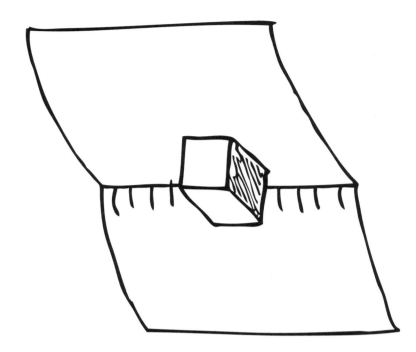

6   Draw a person or an animal or anything you like on another piece of paper and cut it out. Your figure can be a little bit wider and taller than the strip you have made.

7   Put some glue on your strip and stick your figure onto it. Make sure the bottom edge of your figure is on the same line as the bottom edge of the strip, otherwise the card will not open and close properly.

8   Take the piece of card or paper you put to one side. This is now the outside of your card. Glue your card with the strip to the paper. When you open your card, the little figure you cut out will pop up.

9   Finally decorate the front and inside of your card.

¿Cómo se hace?

1   *Tomad dos hojas de papel.*
2   *Cortad la sección pop-up.*
3   *Abrid la tarjeta.*
4   *Dibujad un animal o una persona.*
5   *Pegad el dibujo.*
6   *Decorad la tarjeta.*

You can make a whole range of cards for various occasions by making different designs for the central pop-up piece. Here are some examples with appropriate greetings in Spanish.

Get well soon: *¡Que te mejores pronto!*   Happy Birthday: *¡Feliz cumpleaños! ¡Feliz día!*

Good luck: *¡Buena suerte!*   Congratulations: *¡Felicidades!*

Have a good trip: *¡Buen viaje!*   Happy Christmas: *¡Feliz Navidad!*

Thank you: *¡Muchas gracias!*

Language activities

Activity one: *Happy Birthday to You* song

Practise the Spanish equivalent of the *Happy Birthday* song to the same tune as the English version by singing *Cumpleaños feliz* four times (the words fit the tune better in reverse order!). Make a simple card template for a cake (you could use the pizza template in Chapter 14 for example), draw out the name of a child in the class randomly and bring him/her to the front. Hold up the cake as if for a birthday party. Work out how old the child is, count in Spanish to that number and then all pretend to blow out candles.

Activity two: months of the year

Write up the names of the months in Spanish in a jumbled form and match them together with the English equivalents: *enero, febrero, marzo, abril, mayo, junio, julio, agosto, septiembre, octubre, noviembre, diciembre*. Sing the names aloud going from a high note to a low note. After a few rounds of singing, ask each child to remember the month of their own birthday in Spanish. Go through the months again with the whole class singing/chanting together. Each child jumps up with their arms in the air on their month and shouts the month name as loud as possible. Keep it fast and fun.

Activity three: *Birthday Runs* game

Children form a circle and sit down facing outwards. Go round the outside of the circle giving everyone one of four Spanish numbers near to the age of the children such as *siete, ocho, nueve, diez*. Practise the question *¿Cuántos años tienes?* and say it together several times. Start the game with everyone saying the question twice and then you call out *Tengo diez años* (or any one of the four ages you have chosen). All of the children with that number age must get up, run around the outside of the circle back to their place. Play this a few times and then as an incentive for good behaviour add an extra bonus: if you call out *Feliz cumpleaños*, the running group have to stop in their tracks and run the opposite way. You can keep stopping and starting them as many times as it suits you.

Activity four: talking about birthday dates

Use this simple question form to ask for dates in Spanish:

¿Cuándo es tu cumpleaños?

There are a few simple things to remember about Spanish dates. Firstly, use *the three of May* instead of *the third of May* as in *el tres de mayo*. Secondly always put in the word *de* to mean *of* before the month. Thirdly, the first of the month is expressed as either *el uno de . . .* or *el primero de . . . .* Lastly, the month names don't need a capital letter unless they are the first word in a sentence.

   Make sure the children know the dates of their birthdays and help them put these into Spanish. The teen numbers are *once, doce, trece, catorce, quince, dieciséis, diecisiete, dieciocho, diecinueve*. Twenties numbers start from *veinte, veintiuno, veintidós, veintitrés* etc. and thirty is *treinta* and thirty one is *treinta y uno*. Ask around the class using the model phrase above: *¿Cuándo es tu cumpleaños?* Children reply, for example, *el uno de mayo/el veinte de abril*. When the children are confident with this, they can take their finger puppets and ask each other for their birthday date.

Activity five: make a balloon display

Make a display for the classroom with each child drawing a balloon shape and writing a sentence with their birthday on it, for example, *mi cumpleaños es el tres de mayo*. Note that when you are writing the date in Spanish you just write the number by itself without the extra *th* or *rd* as in *sixth* or *third* in English. Add the balloons to a big collection hanging from a hoop on the ceiling.

Activity six: class birthday chart

As an alternative to the previous activity, each child draws twelve boxes/rectangles on a piece of paper to represent the months of the year. Children label the month boxes in Spanish and ask each other the question: *¿Cuándo es tu cumpleaños?* to find out when each child's birthday falls. When they receive a correct reply such as: *mi cumpleaños es el (catorce de diciembre)*, they write each name on the correct Spanish month and label the whole chart *Mi cumpleaños es . . .*

Chapter 7 at a glance

Dialogue: Mateo and Daniela eat their picnic and talk about the animals they see in the park

Language focus: animals and their habitats

Creative art: make a half-and-half book

Language activities

Activity one: identifying animals

Activity two: matching animals and habitats

Activity three: *Join the Team* team game

Activity four: playing with animals and colours

Activity five: *Carlos the Chameleon* poem

7 Los animales

Animals

Daniela: Estamos en el parque. ¿Qué hora es? Tengo hambre.

Mateo: Son las doce. Tengo hambre y tengo sed. Quiero comer el picnic.

Daniela: Como una manzana. ¿Y tú?

Mateo: Bebo un Coca Cola y como un pastel.

Daniela: Mira, Mateo, debajo del árbol. ¿Qué es eso? ¿Un mono?

Mateo: No, es un conejo. ¿Dónde vive?

Daniela: Vive en un agujero. ¿Y qué es eso en las ramas? ¿Es un panda?

Mateo: No, es un pájaro. Vive en un nido. ¿Y en el agua? ¿Qué es eso? ¿Es un cocodrilo?

Daniela: No, es un pato. ¿Y en la hierba? ¿Es una rata!

Mateo: ¿Y Luna? Vive en la casa!

Luna: ¡Guau! ¡Guau!

(Did you spot the unusual Spanish spelling of *un cocodrilo* for the English *crocodile*?)

Creative art: make a half-and-half book/*hacer un libro en dos partes*

A half-and-half book is a page contributed to by each child and which is divided into an upper and lower half. When each page is complete, a whole book can be put together and the pages cut across the middle to make a mismatching book. The example given is about an animal and its habitat, but could easily be adapted to many other topics such as: an animal and its food, for example, a rabbit eats carrots; a room of the house and something you would do there, for example, in the kitchen I eat my breakfast; something to eat that goes with something else to eat, for example, fish and chips; going somewhere by a particular means of transport, for example, going to school by bus. A finished book is in the colour-plate section.

Resources: one piece of A4 card per child; colouring pencils; spiral binding or treasury tags; pair of scissors.

Steps

1 Lightly draw a line halfway down one piece of A4 card of any colour across the page to divide the page into two sections.
2 In the top half, children draw an animal to fill up the space, colour it in a lively way and label it in Spanish to say, for example, *un perro vive . . .* (a dog lives . . .).
3 In the bottom half, draw the habitat of the animal, colour it and label it in Spanish, for example, *en la selva* (in the jungle).
4 Encourage the children to draw different animals from each other – even birds or fish, as long as they know the target language for them (a small class dictionary might help here and you will need some suggestions up your sleeve too!). Try to get 30 different species from the class! Similarly, try to accumulate different habitats – there are ten in the list below.

English	Spanish
in the desert	*en el desierto*
on the farm	*en la granja*
the air	*en el aire*
in the sea	*en el mar*
in the forest	*en el bosque*
at home	*en la casa*
in the zoo	*en el zoo*
in a tree	*en un árbol*
underground	*bajo tierra*
in a nest	*en un nido*

5 Collect all the finished card pages and assemble in a mixed order so that you have a jumble of different animals rather than all the fish together.
6 Make a front cover, for example *¿Dónde vives?* (Where do you live?) Include a good animal picture too from a child. You may also want to add a strong piece of plain card at the end to keep the book together.

7 If you have access to a spiral binder, use it to put the book together. If not, make four holes down the left side of the pages with a strong hole punch and attach all the pages and covers with treasury tags.

8 With a strong pair of scissors, carefully cut along the midway lines of each page, but not the front and back covers, to separate each page into its two halves.

9 You should now have a half-and-half funny book of matches and mismatches of animals and their habitats.

10 Open the book at any animal and then turn the lower sections to find a 'wrong' habitat.

11 Choose a couple of children to find random animals and habitats every day and read them aloud.

¿Cómo se hace?

1 *Dividid la página en dos partes.*
2 *Dibujad un animal.*
3 *Dibujad el habitat del animal.*
4 *Mezclad las páginas.*
5 *Cortad las páginas en dos partes.*

Language activities

Activity one: identifying animals

Collect all the animal names from the text and identify their English names. Practise the new question *¿Qué es eso?* meaning *What is it?* Then hold up an animal picture card and ask *¿Qué es eso?* Children reply *Es un conejo* . . . Once the children have mastered the *¿Qué es eso?* try to use it as often as possible and even challenge them to learn to spell it.

Activity two: matching animals and habitats

Match up the animals and their habitat names from the text. Ask the question *¿Dónde vive un conejo?* meaning *Where does a rabbit live?* and steer them to the answer *Un conejo vive en un agujero*. Then create some silly habitats for them and put them together such as *un perro vive en el agua, un pájaro vive en el mar, etc*. Draw pictures and label them in Spanish.

Activity three: *Join the Team* team game

Give everyone a small familiar animal card with the Spanish name on it. Have enough to make five or six groups of animals in total in the classroom. The children go around the room, whispering the name of their animal and join up with others of the same name. You can then use these teams for playing further language games, for example the *Conejo* team, the *Perro* team, etc. As an extension to this, ask the children to move around like the animal in whose team they are. Say: *corred como un conejo* – run like a rabbit and the rabbit team does this; *andad como un perro* – walk like a dog and the dog team does this; *volad como un pájaro* – fly like a bird; *nadad como un pato* – swim like a duck. A simpler command is just: *como un conejo, como un perro*, etc. – like a rabbit, like a dog, etc.

Activity four: playing with animals and colours

Choose one of the animals and make it a different colour each time you write a sentence. Add a new habitat for it each time, for example: *un pájaro azul vive en un nido; un pájaro rojo vive en un agujero.* Draw a collection of all your birds/rabbits, etc. in their home and colour and label.

Grammar note: remember that all colours come after the animal name in Spanish, for example, *un perro negro.* A feminine animal such as *una vaca* needs a feminine adjective, such as *una vaca blanca.* Keep to the masculine animals in the dialogue and you are fine.

Activity five: *Carlos the Chameleon* poem

Here is a short poem you could say together about Charles/Carlos the chameleon and where he lives. Children colour in the picture of Charles/Carlos, paste it onto a lollipop stick and then hold up the correctly coloured picture when they hear the relevant habitat.

English   *Charles the chameleon: where do you live?* By Cathy Watts

I am pink. I live in the flowers.
I am yellow. I live on the beach.
I am brown. I live on the farm.
I am silver. I live in the air.
I am blue. I live in the sea.
I am green. I live in the forest.
I am black. I live underground.

Spanish   *Carlos el cameléon: ¿Dónde vives?* By Cathy Watts

Soy rosa. Vivo en las flores.
Soy amarillo. Vivo en la playa.
Soy marrón. Vivo en la granja.
Soy de plata. Vivo en el aire.
Soy azul. Vivo en el mar.
Soy verde. Vivo en el bosque.
Soy negro. Vivo bajo tierra.

Children could recite the dialogue with a group or in a pair saying each line and making up their own colour based on the poem above. Ask the children to practise short dialogues in small groups with their coloured puppets of Charles/Carlos. Here is an example:

English	Spanish
What colour are you?	*¿De qué color eres?*
I am blue.	*Soy azul.*
Where do you live?	*¿Donde vives?*
I live (on the farm).	*Vivo (en la granja).*

Chapter 8 at a glance

Dialogue: Mateo goes for a walk in the woods and finds a monster hiding!

Language focus: numbers and parts of the body

Creative art: make a paper monster

Language activities

Activity one: the monster speaks

Activity two: describing monsters

Activity three: *Join the Body Parts* game

Activity four: *Parachutes* body game

Activity five: monster conversations

Activity six: speech bubbles

8 En el bosque

In the wood

Mateo: Yo voy a jugar con mi perro en el bosque. ¡Hasta pronto!

Daniela: ¡Vale! ¡Ten cuidado! Voy a escalar el árbol.

Mateo: Luna, pórtate bien. ¡Dios mío! Hay muchos árboles. El bosque está tranquilo, muy tranquilo. El bosque está oscuro, muy oscuro.

¡Tengo miedo! ¿Qué es eso? ¿Un monstruo? Tiene una cabeza, dos brazos, dos piernas . . . ¡Socorro! ¡Tengo miedo! ¡Es un monstruo enorme!

Creative art: make a paper monster/*hacer un monstruo*

Monster-making is something all children enjoy and it is amazing how many different varieties of monster they can create!

   Resources: cardboard; butterfly pins (split pins); coloured crayons; decorations (sequins, etc.).

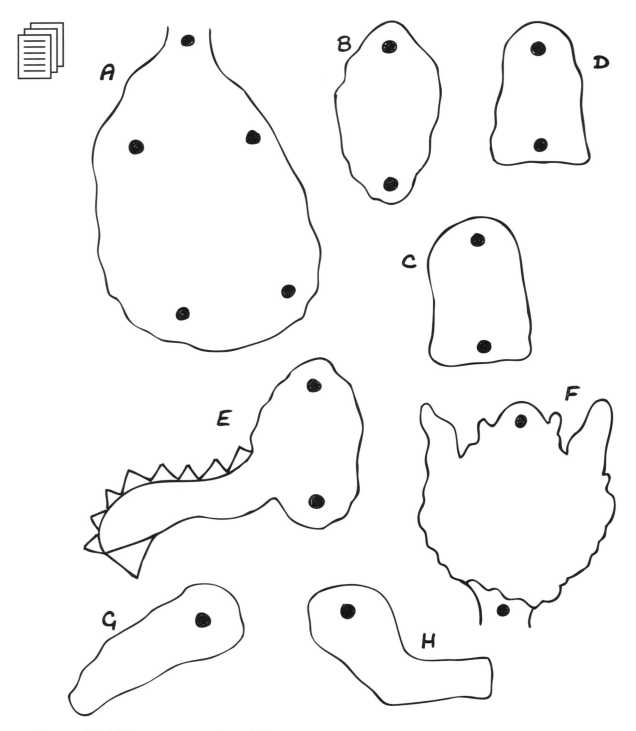

Figure 8.1 Make a monster template

© 2015, *Bringing Spanish to Life*, Catherine Watts and Hilary Phillips, Routledge

Key

A = body

B = upper leg (right)

C = lower leg (right)

D = lower leg (left)

E = upper leg (left) and tail

F = head

G = arm (right)

H = arm (left)

Steps

1 Enlarge and photocopy a monster template for each of the children onto some plain cardboard. Cut out each part of the template (if you put these in an envelope as you finish each template, there is less chance of a piece getting lost).
2 Using a hole punch, make a hole over each of the black spots.
3 Children add eyes, paws, feet, noses, tails, arms, mouths, teeth, spots, scales, etc. This website has some great ideas for drawing eyes, mouths and hair: www.expressivemonkey. com.
4 Colour in, paint and/or decorate the monster according to taste.
5 Attach each monster body part to the correct piece using butterfly pins to make up the whole monster. Flatten out the pins at the back to hold the parts together. The body parts should be attached BEHIND the body not on the front of it.
6 Attach a short piece of string to the top of the monster's head to hang it up with.
7 The body parts around the butterfly pins will be moveable. Each child displays their monster describing how many eyes, teeth, tails, etc. it has. The completed monsters make a great display with some key language running alongside.

¿Cómo se hace?

1 *Cortad las partes del monstruo.*
2 *Añadid los ojos, la boca, los pies, los dientes, las escamas* (scales)*, la cola* (tail) etc. (point to each body part as you say the word in Spanish to provide a visual clue).
3 *Decorad el monstruo.*
4 *Unid las partes del monstruo.*
5 *Colgad el monstruo.*

Language activities

Activity one: the monster speaks

Make a list of all the things you can say already with your monster. Make up some speech bubbles to write a couple of them. Here are some examples:

Me llamo . . .
Tengo ocho años.
Me gustan los pasteles.
No me gusta la leche.
Me lavo los ojos.

Take your monster around the room saying your favourite speech bubble.

Activity two: describing monsters

Use the verb *tengo* (I have) to describe parts of your monster's body. Pretend you are the monster speaking. Here are some examples:

Tengo dos cabezas – I have two heads
Tengo tres brazos – I have three arms
Tengo cuatro ojos – I have four eyes
Tengo cinco piernas – I have five legs

Activity three: *Join the Body Parts* game

Practise three body part names such as: *la pierna* (leg); *el brazo* (arm); *la cabeza* (head). The children run round the room and have to listen for you to call out a Spanish body part, for example, *la pierna*. They have to join up their own *pierna* – gently – with someone else's *pierna* and then wait until everyone is linked up. You can have a group of people linked together for more fun. After a few rounds, name two body parts together and see how they manage.

Activity four: *Parachutes* body game

This is a simple parachute game. Call out different body parts and ask the children to raise the parachute to that level. For example, if you call out *la cabeza*, the children raise the parachute to their forehead; call out *el brazo* and the children raise the parachute with their arms straight ahead. If you go straight from *los pies* (feet) to *la cabeza* (head) you have a huge momentum with the parachute and generate good cooperative spirit.

Activity five: monster conversations

Using the monsters created in the art section, ask the children to move around the room and have a conversation between their monsters, using some of the questions already practised such as those below:

¿Cómo te llamas?	*Me llamo . . .*
¿Cómo estás?	*Muy bien gracias.*
¿Cuántos años tienes?	*Tengo . . . años.*
¿Dónde vives?	*Vivo en . . .*
¿Tu nariz es azul?	*Mi nariz es . . .*
¿Te gusta el chocolate?	*Me gusta . . ./No me gusta . . .*

Activity six: speech bubbles

The monsters could describe themselves in a more complicated way by adding colours to the body parts and using phrases from earlier dialogues to include what the monster eats and likes. Write five speech bubbles with a short description such as:

Tengo dos dientes rojos.
Tengo tres ojos amarillos.
Tengo hambre.

Me gusta el chocolate caliente.
No me gustan los patos.
Me levanto a las doce.

Can the children extend this language to describe themselves? Everyone writes five details about themselves on a sticky note. The teacher/adult picks one note at random and reads it aloud. Who is it? Can you guess?

Me gusta el chocolate.
No me gustan los plátanos.
Tengo ocho años.
Mí cumpleaños es el uno de abril.
Tengo una hermana y un hermano.
Me llamo . . .

Chapter 9 at a glance

Dialogue: Mateo looks into a shed and meets the park keeper

Language focus: the outdoors

Creative art: make a garden shed

Language activities

Activity one: flashcard game with garden items

Activity two: garden back massage

Activity three: *In My Shed* game

Activity four: *Growing Seeds* action rhyme

Activity five: using outdoor spaces

Activity six: a spell for spring – *un hechizo de primavera*

9 El cobertizo

The shed

Mateo: ¿Dónde estás, Luna? ¿Qué es eso? Luna, Luna . . . Es un cobertizo. Aquí hay una ventana . . . Voy a ver . . . A la derecha, puedo ver una pala. Y a la izquierda, puedo ver una araña grande. ¡Dios mío! . . . Pero en el rincón puedo ver un monstruo enorme. Me está mirando . . . ¡Eso no . . .! ¡Luna!

Monstruo: ¿Qué estas haciendo?

Mateo: Señor Monstruo, yo . . .

Monstruo: Soy el guardián del parque. Aquí está tu perro. Es simpático.

Mateo: Gracias, señor. Sé bueno, Luna.

Creative art: make a garden shed/*hacer un cobertizo*

Ask the children to imagine they have a shed in their garden. Some children may really have one that they could describe. What colour would it be on the outside? And on the inside? What would they keep inside their shed?

Resources: one roof and one shed body template for each child photocopied onto cardboard/stiff paper; coloured pencils/crayons/felt pens; glue; glitter (optional).

Steps

1   Using the template on p. 63, cut out enough shed bodies and rooftops (photocopied onto cardboard/stiff paper) for each child to have one set.
2   Each child receives one shed roof and one shed body. Lay them flat and colour the outside of each (white cardboard is easier to colour and decorate). Traditionally, garden sheds are brown, but the children can be as imaginative as possible. Why not have differently coloured door or flowers (*unas flores*) growing up the sides – or even a snail (*un caracol*) near the open window?
3   Fold the roof along the sides and across the middle following the dotted lines. The two triangles at the mid-points on each side need to be glued against the underside of the long fold line. Now glue the apex of each roof so that you have a solid point at the centre of both sides. Glitter (optional) on the roof tops gives a winter shed a lovely frosted finish. Put the roof top to one side while you prepare the body of the shed.

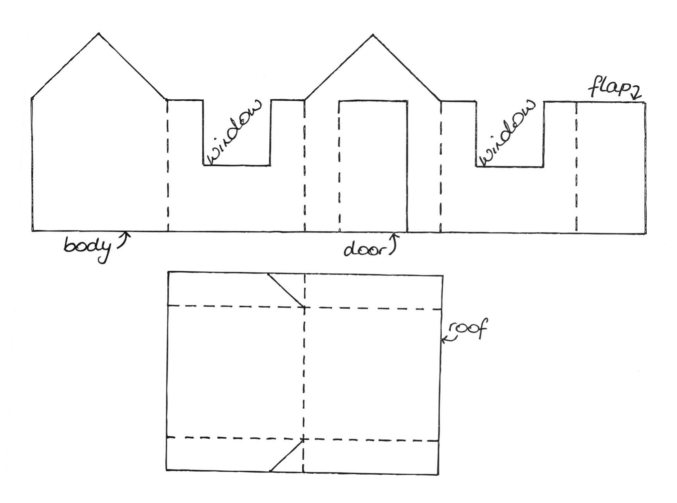

Figure 9.1 Template: a garden shed

© 2015, *Bringing Spanish to Life*, Catherine Watts and Hilary Phillips, Routledge

4   What can you find in a garden shed? Children draw some of the things they would keep in their shed if they had one. They may need to use a bilingual dictionary to research the names of their choices so that they can explain what is inside the shed in Spanish. They should also bear in mind that most garden sheds do not have electricity, so televisions and DVD players are not really appropriate!

5   Fold the flap on the shed body over and glue it to the other side of the shed body to form a neat square with a point above the door and on the back.

6   Now place the roof gently on top of the shed (you can glue it in place with a liquid glue for added security if you like) and your work is finished! When everything is dry, children could ask each other:

Child A: *¿Qué tienes en tu cobertizo?*

Child B: *En mi cobertizo tengo un/una . . .*

¿Cómo se hace?

1   *Coloread el exterior del cobertizo.*
2   *Preparad el techo del cobertizo.*
3   *Dibujad los útiles de jardíneria.*
4   *Doblad el cobertizo en un cuadro.*
5   *Pegad el techo al cobertizo.*

Language activities

Activity one: flashcard game with garden items

Play some flashcard games with pictures of likely (or unlikely) things to find in a garden shed, prompting the answer with *¿Qué es eso?* each time. Games could include showing a quick flash of the picture or just a tiny corner that you slowly increase or hiding a picture behind your back for children to guess. Here are some examples to use for a reply as in: *es una silla*.

a wheelbarrow	*una carretilla*
a watering can	*una regardera*
a chair	*una silla*
a spade	*una pala*
a spider	*una araña*
a broom	*una escoba*
some bulbs	*los bulbos*
some flower pots	*los tiestos*
some seeds	*las semillas*

Grammar note: a plural word would be introduced with *son . . .* as in *son las semillas* or *son las bulbas*.

Activity two: garden back massage

Make a shape to try out on the back of a partner. Children stand or sit in one long line (or in pairs) and trace the shape of one of the objects on the back of the person in front. The partner guesses which object it is. Next, children use their hands to make a series of different shapes on the friend's back, rather like a gentle massage, either reciting the prepared rhyme in unison or speaking one of their own. Here are some examples of what they can do:

Spanish	English
una carretilla	a wheelbarrow

Make lines with the edge of both hands to define the shape

dos arañas	two spiders

Make feathery movements with both hands

tres palas	three spades

Draw firm straight lines

cuatro semillas	four seeds

Make lots of dotting shapes with finger tips all over the back

la lluvia	the rain

Starting at the top of the back, run fingers to waist level

un girasol	a sunflower

Spread hands flat and stroke out in every direction

Activity three: *In My Shed* game

Once you have practised some useful vocabulary, play a game where you have something secret in your shed and children guess what it is. You start with *En mi cobertizo veo . . .* (In my shed I see . . .) and children answer with *es . . . una araña*, etc. This is a good opportunity to bring in a few wild answers that the children may know already such as a lion, a rainbow, an ice cream!

Activity four: *Growing Seeds* action rhyme

Try out an easy action rhyme about something growing like this example:

Spanish	English	Mime
Un paquete de semillas	A packet of seeds	(scatter them on the ground)
Agua	Some water	(use a watering can on the seeds)
Sol	Sunshine	(spread out arms like the sun)
¡Creced! Uno, dos, tres!	Grow, grow one, two, three!	(crouch down and slowly get up again)
¡Y míralo! ¡Un gran girasol!	And there it is! A giant sunflower.	(make a big star jump with wide open arms)

Activity five: using outdoor spaces

Make the most of your outdoor spaces to add a little language to the playground and to any garden areas. Give vegetables and flowers a Spanish label. Children could draw pictures of tools and clothing, such as gloves and wellies, to be hung up with a language label attached and laminated. A bench could have a sign *¡Sentaos!* (Sit down). Special delicate plants and trees could be labelled *¡Andad con cuidado!* (Watch out! Go carefully!)

If you are short of space, put some pots of fast-growing vegetables and flowers on the window ledge in the classroom and label them, for example, *los tomates, las judías, los girasoles* (tomatoes, beans, sunflowers). Next to them make a simple chart of their growth as in the following example (about sunflowers – *los girasoles*): *sembrados el 3 de marzo; cinco centímetros el 30 de marzo; flores blancas el 4 de abril* (planted on 3 March; five cm tall on 30 March; white flowers on 4 April).

Grammar note: if your plants are feminine such as *las judías*, then you would say *sembradas* instead.

Activity six: a spell for spring – *un hechizo de primavera*

Use this example to make a spell to bring on spring

Dos arañas negras	Two black spiders
Un paquete de girasoles	A packet of sunflowers
Una cebolla cortada	A chopped onion
Tres flores blancas	Three white flowers
Un litro de agua sucia	A litre of dirty water
Mezclad bien.	Mix well.
Echad sobre las plantas a las doce de la medianoche.	Pour on the plants at twelve midnight.

Chapter 10 at a glance

Dialogue: Daniela is up a tree watching the pond life

Language focus: insects and pond life/revision of colours

Creative art: make a dragonfly

Language activities

Activity one: animal flashcard game

Activity two: song about insects/animals

Activity three: move like an insect/animal

Activity four: *The Rainbow* poem to revise colours

Activity five: write a nonsense animal or insect poem

Activity six: make an animal or insect bookmark

10 Los insectos

Insects

Mateo:	¿Daniela, dónde estás?
Daniela:	Estoy aquí, en el árbol.
Mateo :	¿Qué estás haciendo en el árbol?
Daniela:	Estoy mirando los insectos cerca del lago. Ven, Mateo, sin hacer ruido.
Mateo:	Mira, aquel insecto grande por allí. ¿Qué es eso?
Daniela:	Es una libélula.
Mateo:	Tiene dos alas grandes.
Daniela:	Claro. Puede volar muy rapidamente.
Mateo:	Y aquel insecto pequeño en tu jersey. ¿Qué es eso?
Daniela:	¡Calla! Es una mariquita. Trae suerte.
Mateo:	Puedo ver tambien una abeja y muchas mariposas. Me encantan las mariposas.
Daniela:	¡Y una rana en el borde!
Mateo:	¡Que monstruo!

Creative art: make a dragonfly/*hacer una libélula*

These are really effective, especially with glitter on their wings, and the completed dragonflies can be suspended around the classroom or even above your own classroom pond. They certainly make an eye-catching display! There are two completed ones in the colour-plate section based on an original design by Cathy Watts at www.pondlifebooks.co.uk.

Resources per child: a traditional wooden clothes peg – the type with two 'legs' and no central clip; one pipe-cleaner; a pair of googly eyes; a wing template; glue; paint – blue and/or green are really effective; glitter (optional).

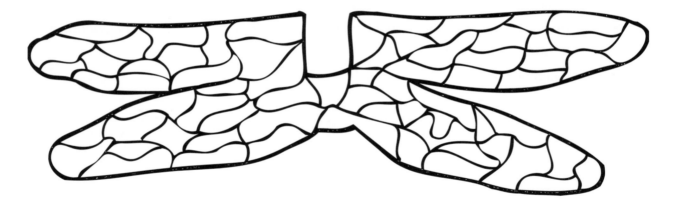

Figure 10.1 Dragonfly-wing template

© 2015, *Bringing Spanish to Life*, Catherine Watts and Hilary Phillips, Routledge

Steps

Preparation: cut out one wing template for each child. The template is the right size to go with a traditional wooden clothes peg.

1   Paint the dragonfly peg body with the paints.
2   Set the body aside to dry (this can be done by putting the pegs onto the rim of a box rather than laying it down on its side, which will smudge the paint).
3   Colour the wings with pencils, pens, etc. on both sides. Or you could use décopatch paper and cover the wings with that, taking care to shave off the overlapping pieces at the end.
4   Glitter can be sprinkled onto the wings at this stage if required. Set the wings aside for a moment to dry out.
5   Stick the two eyes onto the bulge at one end of the peg to make the face. The eyes should touch in the middle.
6   Now cut one pipe-cleaner into three pieces. Make an arch in the middle of each one so it looks rather like a staple. Then bend up the end pieces of each one to make the feet.
7   Place the wings into the slot in the peg.
8   The legs hold the wings in place. Push the arch of each piece of pipe-cleaner underneath the wings and right up to the face-end of the peg. The dragonfly should now be able to stand up on its own – you may need to use a bit of glue to hold the legs firmly in position.
9   Once dry, your dragonfly is ready to be displayed in the classroom!

¿Cómo se hace?

1   *Pintad las partes de la libélula.*
2   *Secad las partes de la libélula.*
3   *Coloread las alas de la libélula.*
4   *Pegad los dos ojos.*
5   *Pegad las alas y las piernas.*

The children could take their dry dragonflies for a short flight around the room/playground. When they meet another dragonfly they could greet it and ask what colour its wings are as in the example below:

Child A: *Hola, Señora Libélula. ¿Estás bien?*
Child B: *Sí, estoy muy bien, gracias. ¿Y tú?*
Child A: *Muy bien, gracias. ¿Eres roja?*
Child B: *No, soy verde, amarilla y roja. ¿Y tú?*
Child A: *Soy negra, azul y blanca.*

Grammar note: *una libélula* (a dragonfly) is feminine in Spanish so our colour descriptions end in 'a' to make a feminine agreement but notice that some adjectives do not change.

Language activities

Activity one: animal flashcard game

Put up pictures of some of the insects and animals in the dialogue (there are a selection overleaf). Now play the flashcard game *Is it this or is it that*? For example, show a dog picture card and ask the children *¿Es una rano o un perro?* (Is it a frog or a dog?) Children reply *Es un perro* (it's a dog).

There are ten pictures below of various common insects and animals. Ask the children to match the correct picture to its name in Spanish.

una rana (a frog)	*una mariposa* (a butterfly)	*una abeja* (a bee)
un gusano (a worm)	*un caracol* (a snail)	*un tritón* (a newt)
una hormiga (an ant)	*una araña* (a spider)	*una mariquita* (a ladybird)
una libélula (a dragonfly)		

© 2015, *Bringing Spanish to Life*, Catherine Watts and Hilary Phillips, Routledge

Plate 1 *Introduction: finger puppets of Mateo and Daniela*

Plate 2 *Introduction: simpler finger puppet*

Plate 3 *Chapter 1: bunting*

Plate 4 *Chapter 2: a paper clock*

Plate 5 Chapter 3: dressed-up figures

Plate 6 Chapter 5: a picnic basket

Plate 7 Chapter 6: a pop-up card

Plate 8 Chapter 7: a half-and-half book

Plate 9 Chapter 8: a monster

Plate 10 Chapter 9: a shed

Plate 11 *Chapter 10: a dragonfly*

Plate 12 *Chapter 10: a bookmark*

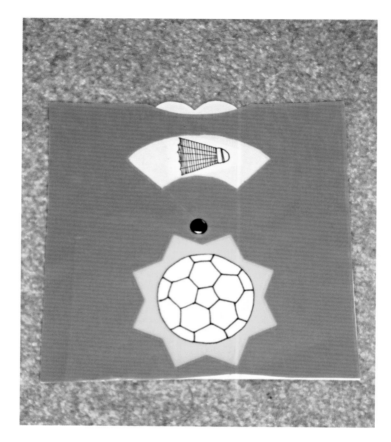

Plate 13 *Chapter 11: a sports wheel*

Plate 14 *Chapter 12: a weather vane*

Plate 15 *Chapter 13: a treasure box*

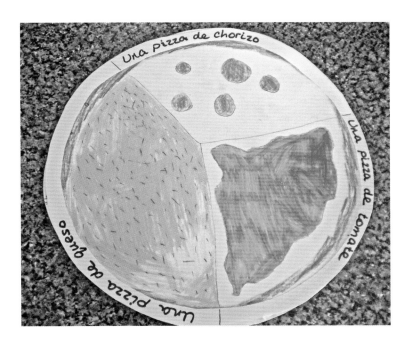

Plate 16 *Chapter 14: a paper pizza*

Plate 17 Chapter 14: a door hanger

Plate 18 Final word: a puppet theatre

Activity two: song about insects/animals

Sing this song about insects in the park song to the tune of *Here we go gathering nuts in May*, walking or skipping around in a circle and then moving on the spot for the final words of each verse.

> Verse one
>
> *Una abeja puedo ver – en el parque, en el parque*
> *Una abeja puedo ver – zum, zum, zum*   (Move on the spot like a bee)
>
> Verse two
>
> *Una libélula puedo ver – en el parque, en el parque*
> *Una libélula puedo ver – ¡Allí arriba!*   (With ending *¡Allí arriba!* point in different directions and hover like a dragonfly.)
>
> Verse three
>
> *Una rana puedo ver – en el parque, en el parque*
> *Una rana puedo ver – ¡dad saltos! [sung as 'dad – sal – tos']*   (Jump round like a frog)

Children could copy out one line of the song, illustrate and label it.

Activity three: move like an insect/animal

Children find a space to stand. Ask them to run – *corred*; walk – *andad*; dance – *bailad*; jump – *saltad*; fly – *volad*; swim – *nadad* and then stop – *parad*. Next ask them to do these movements like the animal and insects from the text, for example, *corred como una libélula, andad como una mariposa*. Extend this with the adverbs slowly – *lentamente* and quickly – *rápidamente*. After some practice, invite a volunteer to take your place.

Activity four: *The Rainbow* poem to revise colours

Here is a simple poem about the colours of the rainbow (with a certain amount of poetic licence as far as the colours are concerned) that you could learn together. Have a set of colour flashcards for volunteers to hold up when their colour is called out. On the last line, each person raises their colour card in turn to make the arc shape, moves both arms in the air from one side to the other and calls out the final words together.

The rainbow	*El arco iris*
Here's the blue	*Aquí está el azul*
Here's the red	*Aquí está el rojo*
Here's the yellow	*Aquí está el amarillo*
Here's the green	*Aquí está el verde*
Here's the purple	*Aquí está el morado*
Here's the pink	*Aquí está el rosa*
Here's the orange	*Aquí está el naranja*
And there it is – the rainbow!	*Y allí está - ¡El arco iris!*

Activity five: write a nonsense animal or insect poem

Compose a short nonsense poem following this model: *andad en el parque como un perro* (walk in the park like a dog). Change the word *andad* for any of the movement verbs used earlier such as *bailad*, *corred*, *volad*, etc. Change the animal *un perro* for any insect or animal. You could even change *el parque* for any of the habitats in Chapter 7, for example, *un agujero, el agua*. Make it as silly as possible, for example: *bailad en el agua como una mariposa* (dance in the water like a butterfly).

Activity six: make an animal or insect bookmark

Take one strip of cardboard 18 cm by 6 cm for each child. Colours show up better on white cardboard. Ask the children to draw a pond creature (they could use the ones in Activity one or make their own up) and decorate their bookmark with their name and the number of animals on it, for example, *cinco libélulas*. If you laminate the bookmark it will have a longer life. These colourful bookmarks make great presents for people! A finished one is in the colour plate section of this book.

Chapter 11 at a glance

Dialogue: Daniela, Mateo and Diego play football together in the park

Language focus: talking about different sports and revision of likes/dislikes

Creative art: make a sports wheel

Language activities

Activity one: talking about which sports you like/dislike playing

Activity two: *Listen for the Difference* sport circle game

Activity three: miming sports

Activity four: conduct a survey (*una encuesta*)

Activity five: make a bar chart of class preferences

Activity six: make a poster

11 Los deportes
Sport

Mateo:	¿Qué hora es? Tengo sueño.
Daniela:	Son las tres. ¿Vamos a jugar con Diego? Ahí está en el parque.
Mateo:	Vamos.
Diego:	¡Hola Luna! ¡Hola Daniela! ¡Hola Mateo! ¿Cómo estáis?
Daniela:	Estamos bien. ¿Jugamos al fútbol?
Diego:	Sí, claro. Me gusta jugar al fútbol.
Daniela:	Prefiero jugar al tenis. Me gusta también el bádminton.
Mateo:	No me gusta jugar al fútbol. Y Luna, prefiere quedarse en la cama!
Luna:	¡Guau! ¡Guau!

Creative art: make a sports wheel/*hacer una rueda de deportes*

A sports wheel encourages good communication between students and is also quite simple to make.

    Resources per child: two templates; coloured crayons; glue; one butterfly pin (split pin).

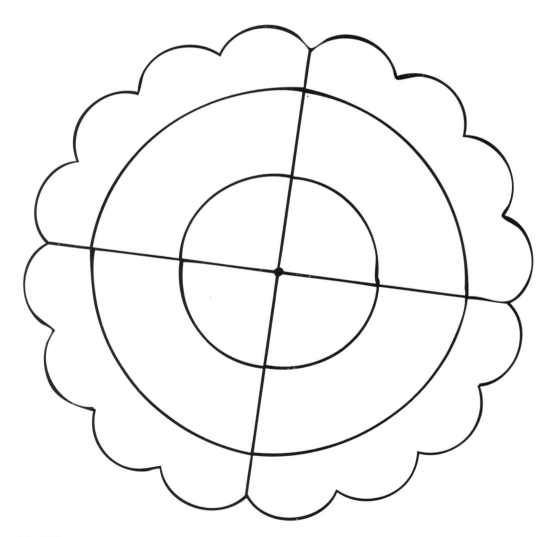

Figure 11.1 Template: sports wheel

© 2015, *Bringing Spanish to Life*, Catherine Watts and Hilary Phillips, Routledge

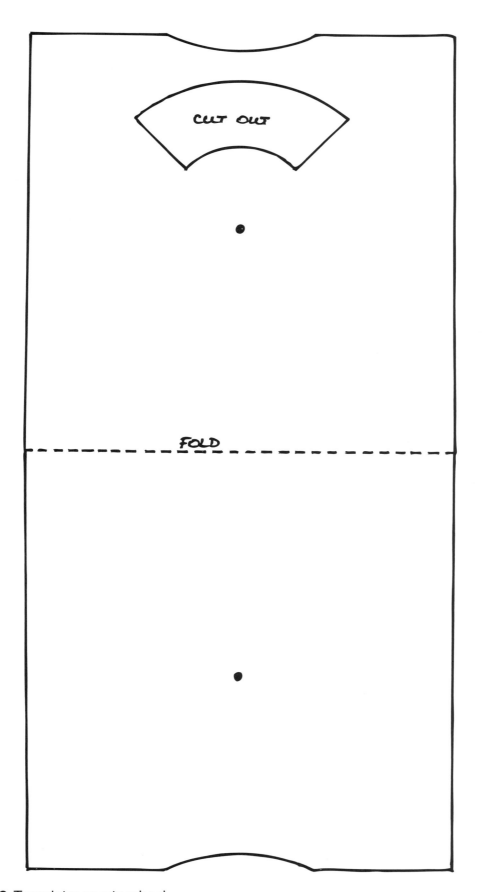

CUT OUT

FOLD

Figure 11.2 Template: sports wheel

© 2015, *Bringing Spanish to Life*, Catherine Watts and Hilary Phillips, Routledge

Steps

1   Photocopy the wheel and the rectangle onto stiff paper or cardboard and give each child a wheel first.
2   In the second circle (not the very inside one) ask the children to draw four symbols representing four sports. Examples could be a tennis racket, a football, a shuttlecock and a cricket bat.
3   Now fold the rectangle along the dotted lines to make the cover for the sports wheel rather like an envelope. Attach the centre points, indicated by the black dots, on the wheel and the cover with a butterfly pin.
4   Glue the tops of the cover, making sure that you can still turn the wheel.
5   Decorate the outside of the cover. Children use their sports wheels to have simple conversations with each other following the model below:

Child A: *¿Te gustan los deportes?*

Child B: *Me gusta el fútbol.*

¿Cómo se hace?

1   *Copiad la rueda y el rectángulo.*
2   *Dibujad cuatro diseños de deportes.*
3   *Doblad el rectángulo.*
4   *Pegad a la rueda.*
5   *Decorad el exterior.*

Language activities

Activity one: talking about which sports you like/dislike playing

Put up pictures of popular sports named below. Practise their names in the usual flashcard way. Revise how to say I like/dislike something: *me gusta/no me gusta*. Put them together with different sports to express preferences such as *me gusta jugar al fútbol/no me gusta jugar al tenis* (I like playing football/I don't like playing tennis). Mime a happy or an unhappy face and then a quick sport action. Children guess what your statement is, for example, *me gusta jugar al bádminton* (I like playing badminton). After a good practice, children play the game in pairs.

Grammar note: in Spanish you have to insert the word *al* before a masculine sport name such as *el fútbol* when you use the word *jugar* (to play). You do not need it just to say if you like or dislike a sport as in *me gusta el fútbol/no me gusta el tenis* (I like football/I don't like tennis). Other sports could be: *jugar al tenis de mesa* (table tennis); *jugar al críquet; jugar al rugby; jugar al bádminton; jugar al hockey.*

Activity two: *Listen for the Difference* sport circle game

Play a tapping game. Children sit in a circle on the floor. One child goes round the outside of circle, tapping each person on the back softly and saying *juego al fútbol* meaning I play football each time. At some point they say instead *juego al tenis* or *juego al bádminton*, etc. The person they touch at that moment gets up and they chase each other round the circle back to that place. Then the winner starts again.

Activity three: miming sports

Play a more varied pretend tennis game. Face the class who are all standing in a space in front of you. Call out *juego al tenis*, play a dramatic miming shot and they return it dramatically repeating the phrase. Switch to a different sport such as *juego al rugby/juego al críquet*, etc., and they continue to copy you with a different mime and phrase. After a few turns, see if you can catch them out: say one sport but mime the wrong one. They must only copy you if both match. They continue in pairs.

Activity four: conduct a survey (*una encuesta*)

Children go round the class individually making a survey of class sport preferences by asking each other the question *¿Qué deporte te gusta?* (Which sport do you like?) expecting the answer *Me gusta el hockey*, etc. . . . and entering the information on a survey sheet with the sports named in Spanish.

Activity five: make a bar chart of class preferences

Make a simple bar chart of sports preferences in the class and label the sports in Spanish. Put the totals for each sport on a label in Spanish too and the title *Los deportes favoritos de la clase* . . .

Activity six: make a poster

Make a sports poster on a piece of A3 paper. Draw different sports (or cut them out of old magazines) and label them in Spanish. One child writes whether or not s/he likes that sport and signs his/her name below the quote.

Chapter 12 at a glance

Dialogue: Daniela, Mateo and Diego discuss the weather in the park

Language focus: talking about the weather and compass points

Creative art: make a weather vane

Language activities

Activity one: weather song

Activity two: weather action rhyme

Activity three: weather actions – whole body response

Activity four: find the compass points

Activity five: a weather forecast

Activity six: fashion parade

12 ¿Qué tiempo hace?

What's the weather like?

Daniela: El fútbol es muy divertido, pero hace frío.

Mateo: ¡No, hace calor! Tengo sed.

Diego: ¡Ay no, está lloviendo! Me llevo una camiseta y un pantalón corto.

Daniela: Tengo un paraguas.

Mateo: ¡Y ahora hace calor! Hace sol. Tengo unas gafas de sol. Y allí está un arco iris para tu cumpleaños, Diego.

Diego: ¡Fantástico!

Creative art: make a weather vane/*hacer una veleta*

The wind brings us our weather, so having a weather vane can be very useful as well as fun to make! There is a completed weather vane in the colour-plate section.

  Resources per child: template arrow head and tail; scissors; ruler; glue; drinking straw; pencil with new rubber on one end; long, straight pin; recycled empty paper cup or yoghurt carton (small); cardboard; pebbles/small stones (optional).

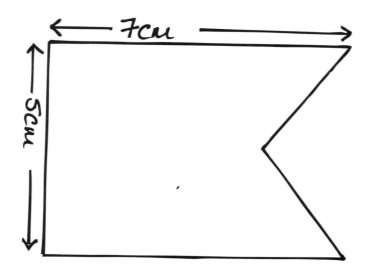
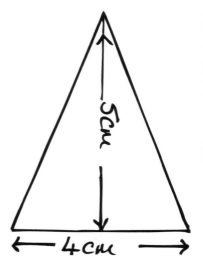

Figure 12.1 Templates: weather vane

© 2015, *Bringing Spanish to Life*, Catherine Watts and Hilary Phillips, Routledge

Steps

1   Cut out the arrow head from the cardboard using the template. It should be 5 cm long and 4 cm wide.
2   Cut out the arrow tail from the cardboard using the template. This should be 7 cm long and 5 cm wide.
3   Make a slit 1 cm long in each end of the drinking straw. Slot the arrow head into the slit at one end and the tail into the other end.
4   Push the pin through the middle of the drinking straw and into the rubber on the end of the pencil.
5   Now turn to your paper cup or yoghurt carton. Decorate it first if you want to. Keeping it right side up, cover the top with a piece of paper. Make four small triangles out of the cardboard and label them N, S, W and E for the wind directions. Stick these onto the cup covering.
6   Push the pointed end of the pencil through the cup/carton cover. Make sure the straw is not too tight so that it turns easily in the wind. Fill the cup with small stones or pebbles to stop it blowing over.
7   Take your weather vanes outside and see which way the wind is blowing!

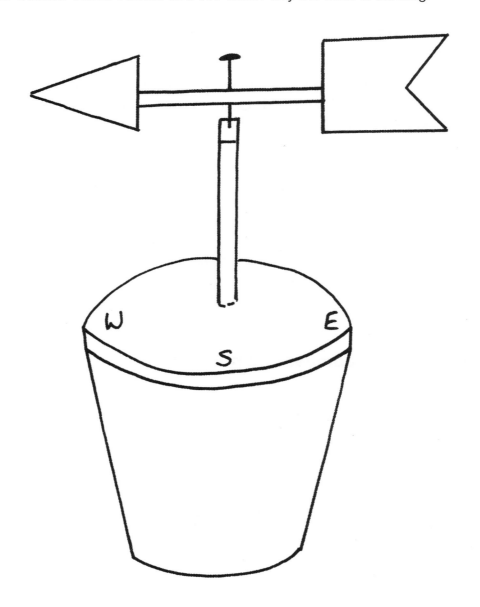

¿Cómo se hace?

1   *Cortad la flecha en cartón.*
2   *Haced un agujero en la pajita.*
3   *Decorad el envase.*
4   *Llenad el envase de piedras.*
5   *¡Buscad el viento!*

Language activities

Activity one: weather song

Bring a group of children out to the front of the class with a weather picture each showing weather for *hace frío/hace calor/está lloviendo/está nevando/hace sol* (it's cold, hot, raining, snowing, sunny). Point to each card in turn and sing the words to the tune of *Frère Jacques*. When you get to the end of the song, close your eyes, ask the children to change places and then sing a totally new version of the song.

Activity two: weather action rhyme

Make up a simple weather rhyme complete with actions such as raindrops falling, shivering with cold. Here are some examples: *hace frío* (shiver); *hace calor* (wipe sweaty brow); *está lloviendo* (raindrops); *está nevando* (wave hands from side to side for snow); *uno, dos, tres, hace sol* (make a big sun in the sky). Practise line by line and then stand up and perform the rhyme in unison. Groups or pairs could then perform their own.

Activity three: weather actions – whole body response

Children run around the room and then repeat the weather you call and perform prepared actions such as *hace frío* – jump up and down vigorously to keep warm; *hace calor* – stretch arms up high and legs to each side as much as possible to keep cool; *está lloviendo* – crouch down as low as possible but keep running to minimise the rain; *está nevando* – stand still as a snowman and count the four buttons on their chest in unison in Spanish; *hace sol* – lie down flat on the ground as if sunbathing.

Activity four: find the compass points

Practise the four basic compass points: *el norte* – north; *el sur* – south; *el este* – east; *el oeste* – west and put up cards on the wall in the correct direction. Children stand in a space and face the front. Call out the direction, for example *el norte*, and children swing round like soldiers to that spot. Keep going and then encourage children to work in pairs or small groups to give each other directions.

Activity five: a weather forecast (*el tiempo de hoy*)

Children work in pairs or independently to work out a weather forecast for the next day or week using both compass points and weather expressions. They could also add the days of the week:

lunes (Monday); *martes* (Tuesday); *miércoles* (Wednesday); *jueves* (Thursday); *viernes* (Friday); *sábado* (Saturday); *domingo* (Sunday).

Here is an example: *lunes, en el norte hace frío.* Children come to the front either on their own or as a pair/group and tell the class their forecast, if possible as an impromptu routine. This could turn into a written forecast, illustrated for a display.

Grammar note: you do not need to add a word for 'on' in front of the weekday. Days of the week in Spanish do not have a capital letter unless they are at the beginning of a sentence.

Activity six: fashion parade for four seasons

This activity makes a good performance for a larger audience. Children form four groups. Each group needs either a set of swimming costumes, a set of scarves, a set of hats or a set of warm gloves. They sing this song together to the tune of *We wish you a merry Christmas* and wave their items of clothing when they are called out. Or they could wear one and wiggle in it!

Verse one	*Me voy de vacaciones* x 3	(I go on holiday)
	En el verano	(In summer)
	Me pongo un traje de baño x 3	(I put on a swimming costume)
	En el verano	(In summer)
Verse two	*Me voy de vacaciones* x 3	(I go on holiday)
	En el invierno	(In winter)
	Me pongo mi bufanda x 3	(I put on my scarf)
	En el invierno	(In winter)
Verse three	*Me voy de vacaciones* x 3	(I go on holiday)
	En la primavera	(In spring)
	Me pongo un sombrero x 3	(I put on a hat)
	En la primavera	(In spring)
Verse four	*Me voy de vacaciones* x 3	(I go on holiday)
	En el otoño	(In autumn)
	Me pongo mis guantes x 3	(I put on my gloves)
	En el otoño	(In autumn)

Chapter 13 at a glance

Dialogue: Daniela and Mateo find some lost treasure on the way home

Language focus: directions and shapes

Creative art: make a treasure box

Language activities

Activity one: match up shapes

Activity two: shape song

Activity three: playing a shape-swapping game

Activity four: *Body Shape* game

Activity five: pass the shape parcel

Activity six: make a shape badge

13 Propiedad perdida
Lost property

Mateo: Tengo hambre y mucho sueño. ¿Qué hora es?

Daniela: Son las seis. Es la hora de la cena. ¡Date prisa, Mateo! Debemos ir a casa.

Mateo: Vale, ya voy. Adiós, Diego. ¡Hasta mañana!

Diego: Adiós, vosotros dos, y Luna. ¡Hasta pronto!

Mateo: ¿Está lejos la casa? Tengo sueño.

Daniela: No, se puede andar allí en cinco minutos. Aquí vamos a la izquerda y después todo recto.

Mateo: ¡Qué lata! He perdido mi juguete.

Daniela: ¿Cómo es, tu juguete?

Mateo: Es un rectángulo rojo y azul.

Daniela: Aquí está, aquí al lado. ¿Estás bien ahora?

Mateo: Sí, claro. Pero mira por allí. ¿Qué es eso?

Daniela: No sé. ¿Un tesoro quizás?

Mateo: ¿Qué clase de tesoro? ¿Cómo es, tu tesoro?

Daniela: Es una pequeña joya en forma de cuadrado, es roja y amarilla. Voy a ponerla en mi caja de tesoros.

Mateo: ¡Esto es una verdadera caja de tesoros! ¡Fantástico!

Creative art: make a treasure box/*hacer una caja de tesoros*

Treasure boxes are good fun to make and, like Daniela and Mateo, you can put all sorts of things inside. What will you put in yours? A finished model is in the colour-plate section.

Resources per child: one box template; items to decorate the box with; paint or coloured crayons.

Steps

1   Photocopy the template below onto stiff paper or white cardboard.
2   Paint the box while it is flat any colour you like.
3   Cut along the solid lines.
4   Fold along the dotted lines.
5   Glue tabs A, B, C and D to the inside of the treasure box as you fold it together.
7   Decorate the sides and the lid of the treasure box with anything you like. What will you keep inside it?

¿Cómo se hace?

1   *Pintad la caja de tesoros.*
2   *Cortad las líneas continuas.*
3   *Doblad a lo largo de las líneas de puntos.*
4   *Pegad las etiquetas A, B, C, y D en el interior de la caja.*
5   *Decorad los lados y la superficie de la caja.*

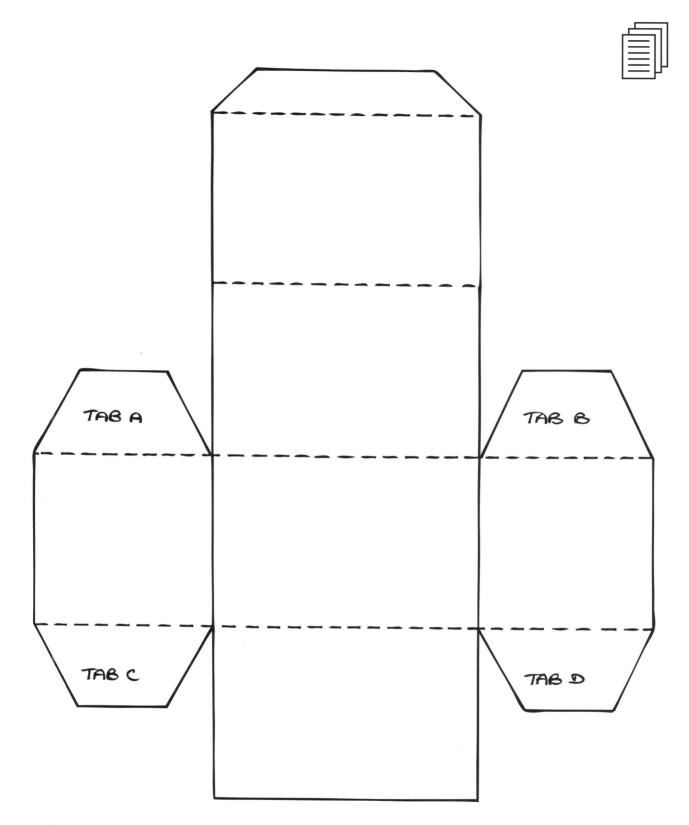

Figure 13.1 Template: a treasure box

© 2015, *Bringing Spanish to Life*, Catherine Watts and Hilary Phillips, Routledge

Language activities

Activity one: match up shapes

Cut out a variety of common 2D shapes in coloured paper and play a match up game with their Spanish shape names. You could use the templates on the next page. Most are easy to recognise, for example *un rectángulo*, *un triángulo, un círculo*, *un rombo*, *un cuadrado* – a square. After practising the shape names, add a colour to the noun and invite children to say the whole phrase.

Question: *¿Cómo es?*

Response: *Es un triángulo verde.*

Activity two: shape song

Sing a simple song to the tune of *Three Blind Mice*, using appropriately coloured shape cards to wave in the air as they sing or drawing the shapes in the air:

Un triángulo verde x 2

Un cuadrado rojo x 2

Un rectángulo azul y blanco x 2

Un círculo naranja x 2

Once children are familiar with the words, ask them to move around the room while singing the words. At the end of the song they find a partner and draw a shape on their partner's back. The partner tries to name the shape. Additional shapes could be *un corazón* – a heart, *una estrella* – a star, *un óvalo* – an oval.

Figure 13.2 Shape templates

© 2015, *Bringing Spanish to Life*, Catherine Watts and Hilary Phillips, Routledge

Activity three: playing a shape-swapping game

In small groups, children have a mixture of different shapes on differently coloured paper. Shuffle the papers and share them out. They ask each other for a particular shape or colour to make a set of their own, for example, a set of blue shapes or a set of triangles of all colours. Here is the question: *¿Tienes un triángulo verde/un cuadrado amarillo? Sí, tengo un cuadrado amarillo/No tengo un triángulo verde.*

Activity four: *Body Shape* game

Ask children to move round the room following the usual warm-up instructions: *¡Corred!/¡Andad!/¡Saltad!* (run/walk/jump) and then call out a number and a shape name. Children should get into groups of that number and try to make that shape on the floor with their bodies. For example, call out *tres niños, un cuadrado*: three children lie on the floor and make one square shape together.

Activity five: pass the shape parcel

Place a selection of familiar shapes of different sizes in a box with a lid or in a drawstring bag. Children sit in a circle on the floor and pass the box/bag around carefully while singing (or chanting) to the tune of *Frère Jacques*:

> *¿Qué es eso?* x 2
>
> *Un triángulo* x 2
>
> *Un cuadrado* x 2
>
> *¿Qué es eso?* x 2

At the end of the song, the child holding the box/bag opens it, pulls out a shape and names it, for example, *es un cuadrado*. The game starts again.

Activity six: make a shape badge

Children make their own coloured shape badges. They choose a shape and draw it onto a piece of coloured paper. They write their favourite word on the badge or perhaps their name or their age or something they like/dislike and the badges are then laminated. Stick a safety pin with tape to the back of the badge so that the children can wear them safely. They go around the room, asking each other about their badges using the phrases they already know such as:

> *¿Qué es eso?*
>
> *Es un cuadrado rojo/un triángulo rojo. Me llamo Rosy. Tengo ocho años. Me gustan las manzanas. No me gusta el chocolate.*

At the end of the conversations, place the badges carefully inside the treasure boxes to use on another day.

Chapter 14 at a glance

Dialogue: pizza flavours

Language focus: preferences and food description

Creative art: make a paper pizza, make a door hanger

Language activities

Activity one: simple pizza song

Activity two: pizza flavour questions

Activity three: *Pizza Circle* game

Activity four: role play pizza shop

Activity five: ordering a pizza

Activity six: likes and dislikes

14 ¡Buen provecho!

Enjoy your meal!

Señora López:	A la mesa, por favor.
Daniela:	¡Tengo mucha hambre!
Mateo:	Yo también.
Señora López:	Esta tarde vamos a comer pizza.
Mateo:	¡Fantástico! Me encanta la pizza. ¡Me gusta la pizza de queso y chocolate!
Daniela:	¡Puaf! Prefiero la pizza de salchichas.
Abuelito:	No me gusta la pizza de jamón y queso. Me gusta mucho la pizza de cuatro estaciones.
Señora López:	Y a mí me gustan todas las pizzas. ¡Buen provecho, toda la familia!

Creative art: make a paper pizza/*hacer una pizza de papel*

You can't really eat these pizzas, but they look great hanging up on display! There's a finished one in the colour-plate section.

Resources: one white paper plate per child or a copy of the template on stiff paper/card; colouring pencils.

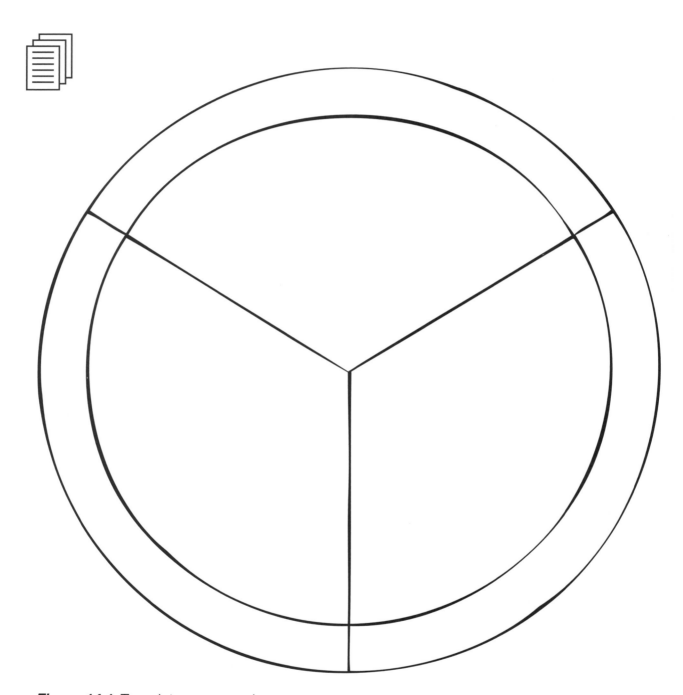

Figure 14.1 Template: a paper pizza

© 2015, *Bringing Spanish to Life*, Catherine Watts and Hilary Phillips, Routledge

Steps

1 Divide the paper plate, if you are using one, into three or four sections.
2 Draw your favourite pizza fillings inside each section.
3 Label each section in Spanish above the filling. Here are some examples:

Una pizza de chorizo
Una pizza de tomate
Una pizza de queso
Una pizza de jamón

4 Once finished, children can ask each other which type of pizza they like using their paper models. Serve with a smile! *¡Buen provecho!*

¿Qué pizza te gusta?
Me gusta la pizza de tomate.

¿Cómo se hace?

1 *Dividid el plato en tres o cuatro secciones.*
2 *Dibujad los ingredientes en cada seccion.*
3 *Coloread la pizza.*
4 *Servid con una sonrisa. ¡Buen provecho!*

Language activities

Activity one: simple pizza song

Sing this song either to the tune of *London Bridge is falling down* or *Here we go gathering nuts in May*. Start with a straightforward repeated phrase several times:

Me gusta la pizza de queso, de queso, de queso
Me gusta la pizza de queso. ¡Buen provecho!

Invite children to suggest a pizza flavour for the next verse. After that, try changing the last line to a side order for example *con ensalada/con patatas fritas*. Children could then work in a small group and sing a verse of their own pizza flavour to the rest of the class, acting out either making or eating the food.

Activity two: pizza flavour questions

Put up the verb prompts *Me gusta/No me gusta/Me encanta . . ./Prefiero . . .* and encourage children to work out their preferences for pizza flavours. Ask the question *¿te gusta la pizza?* to elicit a reply. Children could ask the same question to everyone on their table, for example, *¿Te gusta la pizza de jamón?/No, prefiero la pizza de salchicha.*

Activity three: *Pizza Circle* game

Children stand in a circle with five or six children standing separately at the side, out of earshot. The main group huddle together, decide on a secret number between one and ten and then join hands to raise and lower their arms in the air in a steady rhythm. The separate group return and run in and out of the raised arms of the first group who chant loudly in unison: *¡Me gusta la pizza, sí, sí, sí! ¡No me gusta la pizza, no, no, no!* and then count up to ten in Spanish. When the group reach their chosen number they lower their arms and catch as many of the small group as possible in their net. Any children caught in the net join the larger group and are replaced by others as the game starts again.

Activity four: role play pizza shop

Turn the classroom or hall into a pizza shop for a role play. Half the children take the part of a Pizza Parlour cook while the others become customers. Swap parts after a while. Groups could put up menus of pizza flavours and prices in euros with prompts readily available for key words for example: *Quiero . . ./¿Cuanto cuesta, por favor?/Muchas gracias.* (I would like/How much is it please?/Thanks very much.) Cooks could make very quick headbands from a piece of card with the name of their pizza shop such as *La tienda de Sam/El café de Maddy*. Shoppers move round and order pizzas, using polite phrases to greet each other, for example: *¡Hola Señor/ Señora! Quiero una pizza de queso por favor.*

Activity five: ordering a pizza

Children work in pairs to make up a dialogue between a cook and a customer like those practised above or a telephone conversation ordering a pizza. Confident pairs could perform to the class.

Activity six: likes and dislikes

Children make up a list of the pizzas they like such as *me gusta la pizza de queso* and then a list of pizzas they don't like such as *no me gusta la pizza de jamón*. They can put these two views together using *pero . . .* (but . . .) as in: *me gusta la pizza con queso pero no me gusta la pizza con jamón.*

After supper, it's time for bed. Goodnight Daniela and Mateo – and Luna. See you again soon! *Y ahora a la cama. Buenas noches Daniela y Mateo – y Luna. ¡Hasta pronto!*

Make a door hanger/*hacer un colgadero de puerta*

Steps: this one is easy to make.

1 Copy the template below and decorate it. Here are some useful phrases you could use:

Do not disturb: *¡No molestar!*

No entry: *¡No entrar!*

Silence! I'm thinking: *¡Silencio, estoy pensando!*

Beware, hamster on the loose: *¡Cuidado, el hámster anda suelto!*

2 Laminate the finished hanger and cut a slit in the handle so that it fits on any door.

Figure 14.2 Template: a door hanger

© 2015, *Bringing Spanish to Life*, Catherine Watts and Hilary Phillips, Routledge

Curriculum links

In this book you will find many activities that provide a link to other areas of the curriculum, enabling you to reinforce skills or knowledge in a new language.

Literacy

- Name the appropriate word class (nouns, verbs, adjectives, etc.) as you teach all new vocabulary and display each word class on different colour paper.
- Collect together words of each class in a display on the wall and refer to them as our Spanish noun collection, our Spanish verbs.
- Develop a growing awareness of the structures of the English language and similarities (and differences) to another language such as the use of connectives to join clauses.
- Make short phrases together using a scaffold, identifying the word class such as a pronoun, verb and adverb so *ando lentamente* – I walk slowly. Note that in Spanish the pronoun is not used except for emphasis as in Me, I like chocolate. Children use this scaffold and a list of appropriate alternatives to make their own.
- Play games with words of different classes such as:
  1 Put a collection of words from different classes on the floor. Children pick one at random. Play fruit salad where the nouns change places.
  2 Children join up together to make a noun and a verb, then add an adverb and read the results aloud.
  3 Children make a longer sentence using a connective to join two of the clauses above.
  4 Alternatively, adjectives and nouns join up in the correct order and then add a verb at the beginning such as *Yo veo* – I see to make a sentence.
  5 Instead of words, place letters on the floor and encourage children to form familiar word types such as verbs. Read them aloud together and then make them negative using *no* as in *Yo veo/Yo no veo* – I see/I don't see.
- Develop progression from simple phrases to more complex sentences: from stating simple opinions to linking opposing opinions with a connective; forming and posing a variety of questions and then supplying a suitable answer; making a positive statement and then making it negative.

Drama and creative work

- Repeat and practise phrases, sentences and whole dialogues. Re-enact dialogues as a class exercise, covering up an increasing number of words every time you practise.
- Provide opportunities for drama work in role plays of shopping scenes, fashion parade, pizza shop (Chapter 14) and mini-dialogues in every chapter.

- Provide opportunities for creative work based on a given formula, for example: Chameleon poem based on colours; Garden spell for bringing on spring.
- Encourage reading skills by building up a core of texts written by your class in Spanish as part of your class library, using the half-and-half books activity as a starting point. Put together examples of children's poems to make a class book and choose one each day for a child to read aloud to the class. Children dip into them in free time.

PSHE

- Play circle games where children develop listening and co-operative skills.
- Encourage paired and small group activities where children work together to practise vocabulary, create and perform simple routines.
- Introduce sharing activities where children work together to use equipment they have made such as weather vanes.
- Develop a positive environment by encouraging children to recognise and value other people's achievements.
- Adopt an inclusive approach to language learning. It is generally acknowledged that children with special needs thrive in early language learning because of the emphasis on kinaesthetic activities, oracy skills and a structured approach to learning.

Numeracy

- Try out simple mental calculations in Spanish as oral starters to lessons using four operations: *más* (add), *menos* (minus), *por* (times), *dividido entre* (divided by).
- Reinforce known shape names by repetition in Spanish.
- Revise knowledge of time with use of clock faces and paired work asking and answering time questions.

Science

- Look at food groups and recognise healthy and unhealthy meals using Spanish labels.
- Identify parts of plants, observe and record their growth adding Spanish phrases.
- Reinforce the linking of animals to their habitats.
- Trace the growth of animals such as insects and animals like *la libélula/la rana.*

Geography

- Revise the four basic compass points and expand into eight points by combining directions such as *el sureste, el noroeste.*
- Reinforce weather reports by adding details in Spanish. Use weather vanes to track wind direction.

Music

- Make up a simple Spanish song or rhyme to a familiar tune and sing as a class, in a small group or as a round.
- Children make their own actions to accompany a song or use instruments to enhance the performance.

- Children develop cultural awareness of authentic Spanish songs using commercial CDs.
- Develop a sense of rhythm when practising new vocabulary by clapping or moving hands and arms to fit the shape of a new sentence or phrase.

Physical education

- Use the games described as PE starters involving team work, developing co-operative skills.
- Use authentic Spanish songs to create a mood for mini-dance routines or exercise workouts.
- Find out about teams or players in Spain at the time of international events such as the World Cup.

Art and design

- Children develop art and design techniques by creating the models in each chapter.
- Discuss the impact and style of paintings by Spanish artists such as *Pablo Picasso* and *Joan Miró*.

Mini-puppet theatre

Acting out the dialogues is a fun way to embed the Spanish language in this book. Each dialogue is written like a short play and all the children need to do is to make up the theatre on the next page, stand it on a table top and get talking using their finger puppets to provide the action. Some of the dialogue scenes do not take place in the park, in which case some adjustments to the backdrop will be necessary. A completed mini-theatre is in the colour-plate section. Ten mini-beasts from Chapter 10 are included in the theatre scene – and an extra animal too. Can the children find it?

Steps

1 Colour in the backdrop overleaf and cut it out along the solid lines.
2 Fold along the dotted lines to make the sides of the scene.
3 Using a hole punch, make four holes where indicated on the sides.
4 Place a cloth on the top of a table and stand the scene on it.
5 Choose a dialogue from the book to act out.
6 Organise the finger puppets on each side of the scene.
7 Glue each finger puppet to the end of a drinking straw. Be careful to attach the straw according to whether the character comes from the right or left of the scene.
8 Poke the straws with the finger puppets on the end through the holes and push them on and off the scene using the dialogue to tell the story. At least two children are needed to work the characters on each side of the scene.
9 Play some music as the audience assembles. Are there any other sound-effects you could include?
10 Serve some refreshments such as popcorn between dialogues.
11 Take a bow at the end to the applause!

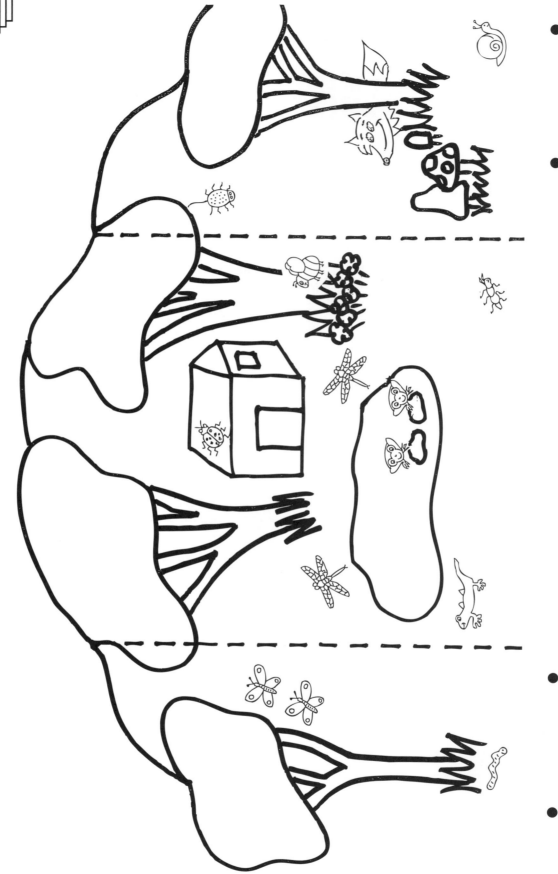

© 2015, *Bringing Spanish to Life*, Catherine Watts and Hilary Phillips, Routledge

Figure A.1 Template: mini-puppet theatre

Translation of dialogues

Chapter 1 Welcome to the López family!

Daniela: Hi! My name is Daniela! What's your name?

Mateo: Hi! My name is Mateo! How old are you? I'm eight.

Daniela: I'm nine years old. I live in Spain with my mother, my grandfather and my brother.

Mateo: That's me! I am your brother. And my sister. That's you, Daniela!

Daniela: Yes, I'm your sister. And here is our dog Luna.

Mateo: How are you? I'm very well. We're on our summer holidays.

Daniela: Me too, I'm fine. I love the holidays. Welcome to the López family!

Chapter 2 What time is it?

Mateo: What time is it?

Daniela: It's seven o'clock.

Mateo: Oh no, it can't be! I'm asleep.

(one hour later)

Mateo: What time is it?

Daniela: It's eight o'clock.

Mateo: Oh no! It's the summer holidays. I'm staying in bed!

(one hour later)

Mateo: What time is it?

Daniela: It's nine o'clock. Get up!

Mateo: I'm getting up. I'm hungry.

Daniela: Yes it's time for breakfast. Afterwards I'm going to the park.

Mateo: Me too. I'll play with Luna.

Chapter 3 I get up

Daniela: I'm getting up and I'm washing my ears.

Mateo: And I'm washing my eyes and my nose.

Daniela: Then wash your hands!

Mateo: Yes, I'm washing my hands. And you wash your feet!

Daniela: OK, I'll wash my feet. Brush your teeth!

Mateo: Yes, I'm brushing my teeth. You brush your hair.

Daniela: Yes, I'm brushing my hair. And now I'm getting dressed. Put on your shorts, Mateo.

Mateo: I'm putting on my blue shorts and a red jumper.

Daniela: And I'm putting on green shorts and a yellow t-shirt. Let's go!

Chapter 4 Breakfast

Daniela: What's the time?

Mateo: It's nine o'clock. It's breakfast time. I'm hungry.

Daniela: And I'm thirsty. I'm drinking hot chocolate and eating some toast.

Mateo: I don't like hot chocolate. I like milk. I'm a milk monster!

Daniela: Do you like cereal?

Mateo: Yes, I love cereal. Do you like churros?

Daniela: No, I don't like churros. I prefer sandwiches.

Mateo: Enjoy your meal!

Chapter 5 The picnic

Grandad: Good morning Mateo. How are you? Where are you going?

Mateo: I'm fine, Grandad. I'm going to the park with Daniela and Luna to have a picnic.

Grandad: Here are ten euros to buy some picnic things. One euro, two, three, four, five, six, seven, eight, nine, ten euros! There you are!

Mateo and Daniela: Thank you very much Grandad. Let's go! See you later!

(at the market)

Shopkeeper: Good morning children. What would you like?

Daniela: Good morning Señor. I'd like two apples please.

Shopkeeper: Anything else?

Mateo: Two bananas please.

Shopkeeper: Anything else?

Daniela: Two tomatoes please.

Shopkeeper: Anything else?

Mateo: Two strawberry tarts and two cokes please.

Daniela: How much is that please?

Shopkeeper: That's five euros.

Daniela: Here you are Señor. Thank you. Goodbye!

Chapter 6 Happy birthday!

Daniela:	The park is close by. But look, Mateo, there's our cousin Diego.
Diego:	Hi Daniela and hi there Mateo! How are you?
Mateo:	I'm great thanks. Is it your birthday today?
Diego:	Yes, it's today, it's the third of March.
Mateo:	How old are you?
Diego:	I'm ten.
Mateo:	I don't have a birthday card for you! I'm sorry.
Daniela:	But we've got a strawberry tart with one candle.
Daniela and Mateo:	Happy Birthday!
Luna:	Woof! Woof!

Chapter 7 Animals

Daniela:	Here's the park. What's the time? I'm hungry.
Mateo:	It's midday. I'm hungry and I'm thirsty. I'd like to eat the picnic.
Daniela:	I'll eat an apple. What about you?
Mateo:	I'll drink a coke and eat a tart.
Daniela:	Look Mateo, over there under the tree. What is it? Is it a monkey?
Mateo:	No, it's a rabbit. Where does it live?
Daniela:	It lives in a hole. And in the branches, what's that? Is it a panda?
Mateo:	No, it's a bird. It lives in a nest. And in the water? What's that? Is it a crocodile?
Daniela:	No, it's a duck. And in the grass? It's a rat!
Mateo:	And Luna? He lives in the house!
Luna:	Woof! Woof!

Chapter 8 In the wood

Mateo:	I'm going to play with the dog in the wood. See you soon.
Daniela:	OK. Be careful. I'm going to climb up the tree.
Mateo:	Luna, behave yourself. Oh no, there are lots of trees. The wood is quiet, really quiet. The wood's dark, really dark. I'm frightened . . . What's that? A monster? It's got a head, two arms, two legs . . . Help! I'm scared! It's a huge monster!

Chapter 9 The shed

Mateo:	Luna, where are you? What's that? Luna! Luna! It's a shed. Here's a window . . . I'm going to look inside . . .
	I can see a spade on the right. And on the left I can see a huge spider. But in the corner I can see . . . a huge monster. He's looking at me . . . Oh no! . . . Luna!
The monster:	What are you doing?
Mateo:	Mister Monster I . . .
The monster:	I'm the park keeper. Here's your dog. He's nice.
Mateo:	Thank you Señor. Luna, be good.

Chapter 10 Insects

Mateo:	Daniela, where are you?
Daniela:	I'm up here, in the tree.
Mateo:	What are you doing in the tree?
Daniela:	I'm looking at the insects beside the lake. Come quietly, Mateo.
Mateo:	Look, the big insect over there, what is it?
Daniela:	It's a dragonfly.
Mateo:	It's got two big wings.
Daniela:	Of course, it can fly very quickly.
Mateo:	And the little insect on your jumper, what's that?
Daniela:	Shh! It's a ladybird. They're lucky!
Mateo:	I can see a bee as well and lots and lots of butterflies. I love butterflies.
Daniela:	And a frog at the side!
Mateo:	What a monster!

Chapter 11 Sport

Mateo:	What time is it? I'm tired.
Daniela:	It's three o'clock. Shall we go and play with Diego? There he is in the park.
Mateo:	Let's go.
Diego:	Hi Luna! Hi Daniela! Hi Mateo! How are you?
Daniela:	We're fine. Shall we play football?
Diego:	Yes, OK. I like playing football.
Daniela:	I prefer playing tennis. I like badminton too.
Mateo:	I don't like playing tennis. I prefer football! As for Luna – he'd rather stay in bed!
Luna:	Woof! Woof!

Chapter 12 What's the weather like?

Daniela:	Football's fun, but it's cold.
Mateo:	No it isn't, it's hot! I'm thirsty.
Diego:	Oh no, it's raining. I'm wearing a t-shirt and a pair of shorts.
Daniela:	I've got an umbrella.
Mateo:	And now it's hot again! It's sunny. I've got sunglasses. And there's a rainbow for your birthday, Diego!
Diego:	That's great!

Chapter 13 Lost property

Mateo:	I'm hungry and I'm very, very tired. What's the time?
Daniela:	Oh! It's six o'clock. It's dinner time. Hurry up Mateo. We must go home.
Mateo:	OK. I'm coming. Cheerio Diego. See you tomorrow.
Diego:	Bye, both of you – and Luna. See you soon.
Mateo:	Is it a long way home? I'm tired.
Daniela:	No, five minutes' walk away. It's left here and then straight ahead.
Mateo:	Oh no! I've lost my toy.
Daniela:	What's it like, your toy?
Mateo:	It's a red and blue rectangle.
Daniela:	Here it is, at the side. Is that OK now?
Mateo:	Yes of course. But look over there. What is that?
Daniela:	I don't know. A piece of treasure, maybe?
Mateo:	What treasure? What's your treasure like?
Daniela:	It's a little jewel – it's a square shape in red and yellow. I'm going to put it in my treasure box.
Mateo:	This is a proper treasure hunt! Hooray!

Chapter 14 Enjoy your meal!

Mrs López:	Come and sit at the table please.
Daniela:	I'm starving!
Mateo:	Me too!
Mrs López:	It's pizza tonight.
Mateo:	Fantastic! I love pizza. I like cheese and chocolate pizza!
Daniela:	Yuk! I prefer sausage pizza.
Grandad:	I don't like ham and cheese pizza. I really like four seasons pizza.
Mrs López:	And I like all kinds of pizza. Enjoy your meal everyone!

Taylor & Francis eBooks

eBooks
from Taylor & Francis

Helping you to choose the right eBooks for your Library

Add to your library's digital collection today with Taylor & Francis eBooks. We have over 50,000 eBooks in the Humanities, Social Sciences, Behavioural Sciences, Built Environment and Law, from leading imprints, including Routledge, Focal Press and Psychology Press.

ORDER YOUR FREE INSTITUTIONAL TRIAL TODAY

Free Trials Available

We offer free trials to qualifying academic, corporate and government customers.

Choose from a range of subject packages or create your own!

Benefits for you

- Free MARC records
- COUNTER-compliant usage statistics
- Flexible purchase and pricing options
- 70% approx of our eBooks are now DRM-free.

Benefits for your user

- Off-site, anytime access via Athens or referring URL
- Print or copy pages or chapters
- Full content search
- Bookmark, highlight and annotate text
- Access to thousands of pages of quality research at the click of a button.

eCollections

Choose from 20 different subject eCollections, including:

- Asian Studies
- Economics
- Health Studies
- Law
- Middle East Studies

eFocus

We have 16 cutting-edge interdisciplinary collections, including:

- Development Studies
- The Environment
- Islam
- Korea
- Urban Studies

For more information, pricing enquiries or to order a free trial, please contact your local sales team:

UK/Rest of World: **online.sales@tandf.co.uk**
USA/Canada/Latin America: **e-reference@taylorandfrancis.com**
East/Southeast Asia: **martin.jack@tandf.com.sg**
India: **journalsales@tandfindia.com**

www.tandfebooks.com